CYCLING THE NORTH COAST 500

A CYCLIST-FRIENDLY GUIDE TO SCOTLAND'S NC500

by Mike Wells

JUNIPER HOUSE, MURLEY MOSS,
OXENHOLME ROAD, KENDAL, CUMBRIA LA9 7RL
www.cicerone.co.uk

© Mike Wells 2024
Second edition 2024
ISBN: 978 1 78631 219 8
First edition 2019

Printed in Turkey by Pelikan Basim using responsibly sourced paper.
A catalogue record for this book is available from the British Library.
All photographs are by the author unless otherwise stated.

Route mapping by Lovell Johns www.lovelljohns.com
© Crown copyright and database rights 2019
AC0000810376. NASA relief data courtesy of ESRI

Updates to this Guide

While every effort is made by our authors to ensure the accuracy of guidebooks as they go to print, changes can occur during the lifetime of an edition. Any updates that we know of for this guide will be on the Cicerone website (www.cicerone.co.uk/1219/updates), so please check before planning your trip. We also advise that you check information about such things as transport, accommodation and shops locally. Even rights of way can be altered over time. We are always grateful for information about any discrepancies between a guidebook and the facts on the ground, sent by email to updates@cicerone.co.uk or by post to Cicerone, Juniper House, Murley Moss, Oxenholme Road, Kendal, LA9 7RL.

Register your book: To sign up to receive free updates, special offers and GPX files where available, create a Cicerone account and register your purchase via the 'My Account' tab at www.cicerone.co.uk.

Front cover: The Bealach na Bà mountain pass road (Stage 3A) (photo by Helen Hotson/stock.adobe.com)

CONTENTS

Route summary 6
Suggested schedules 8

INTRODUCTION 11
Background 14
The route 21
Natural environment 23
Preparation. 28
Getting there and back 28
Navigation and information 31
Accommodation. 34
Food and drink 35
Amenities and services 38
What to take. 39
Safety and emergencies 40
About this guide 42

THE ROUTE 43
Stage 1   Inverness to Garve 44
Stage 2   Garve to Lochcarron 51
Stage 3   Lochcarron to Shieldaig (direct route) 56
Stage 3A   Lochcarron to Shieldaig (via Applecross) 61
Stage 4   Shieldaig to Gairloch 65
Stage 5   Gairloch to Ullapool 71
Stage 6   Ullapool to Lochinver 81
Stage 7   Lochinver to Kylesku 89
Stage 8   Kylesku to Durness 93
Stage 9   Durness to Tongue. 98
Stage 10   Tongue to Melvich 104
Stage 11   Melvich to John o' Groats (coastal route) 108
Stage 12   John o' Groats to Melvich (inland route) 117
Stage 13   Melvich to Altnaharra 120
Stage 14   Altnaharra to Tain 127
Stage 12A   John o' Groats to Lybster 136
Stage 13A   Lybster to Brora 142
Stage 14A   Brora to Tain 148
Stage 15   Tain to Nigg (for Cromarty ferry) 154
Stage 16   Cromarty to Inverness 158

Stage 15A Tain to Dingwall 164
Stage 16A Dingwall to Inverness 170

Appendix A	Facilities summary 173
Appendix B	Tourist information 180
Appendix C	Hostels and bunkhouses 181
Appendix D	Campsites 184
Appendix E	Cycle shops and cycle hire 188
Appendix F	Munros near route (mountains over 914m) 190
Appendix G	Distilleries en route 192
Appendix H	Useful contacts 194

Foreword

This guidebook to cycling in Scotland's far north describes a route that circumnavigates the northern Highlands and visits Scotland's wild and remote western, northern and eastern coasts from a start and finish point in Inverness. It mostly follows the signposted NC500 (North Coast 500), which is a route designed for motorised tourists using cars, camper vans, caravans or motorbikes. This can be followed by cyclists but sections on busy main roads with fast-moving traffic make this a potentially risky undertaking. In this book almost all of the NC500 is described with the addition of recommended alternative, more cycle-friendly, routes that avoid both the most dangerous parts and the steepest hills.

Acknowledgements

Many thanks to all at Ticket to Ride cycle hire and cyclist transport provider in Inverness for their help in researching this guide

Abandoned croft near Bettyhill (Stage 10)

CYCLING THE NORTH COAST 500

ROUTE SUMMARY

Stage	Start	Finish	Via	Distance miles (km)	Ascent (m)	Descent (m)	Page
1	Inverness	Garve		24.5 (39.5)	237	189	44
2	Garve	Lochcarron		36.5 (58.5)	214	281	51
3	Lochcarron	Shieldaig	direct route	15.5 (25)	301	302	56
3A	Lochcarron	Shieldaig	Applecross	42.5 (68.5)	1292	1293	61
4	Shieldaig	Gairloch		36.5 (58.5)	597	589	65
5	Gairloch	Ullapool		55 (88.5)	1078	1081	71
6	Ullapool	Lochinver		35.5 (57)	606	611	81
7	Lochinver	Kylesku		24.5 (39.5)	770	749	89
8	Kylesku	Durness		35 (56.5)	714	699	93
9	Durness	Tongue		29.5 (47.5)	596	591	98
10	Tongue	Melvich		27.5 (44.5)	744	781	104
11	Melvich	John o' Groats	coastal route	35.5 (57)	396	399	108

Route summary

Stage	Start	Finish	Via	Distance miles (km)	Ascent (m)	Descent (m)	Page
12	John o' Groats	Melvich	inland route	36.5 (58.5)	432	429	117
13	Melvich	Altnaharra	inland route	48.5 (78)	445	371	120
14	Altnaharra	Tain	inland route	46.5 (75)	299	354	127
12A	John o' Groats	Lybster	east coast A9	30 (48.5)	345	282	136
13A	Lybster	Brora	east coast A9	33 (53)	618	675	142
14A	Brora	Tain	east coast A9	25 (40)	229	213	148
15	Tain	Nigg (for Cromarty)	using ferry	15 (24)	112	134	154
16	Cromarty	Inverness		26 (42)	416	397	158
15A	Tain	Dingwall	avoiding ferry	23 (37)	255	272	164
16A	Dingwall	Inverness		14.5 (23.5)	201	187	170
Main route total	Inverness	Inverness		**528 (850)**	**7957**	**7957**	

Suggested schedules from Inverness

Miles from Inverness	8 DAYS	10 DAYS	13 DAYS	17 DAYS
Inverness — 0	Inverness to Lochcarron 61 miles ascent 451m	Inverness to Lochcarron 61 miles ascent 451m	Inverness to Achnasheen 40.5 miles ascent 379m	Inverness to Garve 24.5 miles ascent 237m
Muir of Ord				
Garve — 20				Garve to Lochcarron 36.5 miles ascent 214m
Achnasheen — 40			Achnasheen to Torridon 43.5 miles ascent 557m	
Lochcarron — 60				
Shieldaig — 80	Lochcarron to Aultbea 64 miles ascent 1170m	Lochcarron to Gairloch 52 miles ascent 898m		Lochcarron to Kinlochewe 32.5 miles ascent 614m
Torridon				
Kinlochewe — 100			Torridon to Aultbea 41 miles ascent 685m	
Gairloch				Kinlochewe to Aultbea 31.5 miles ascent 556m
Poolewe — 120				
Aultbea				
Dundonnel — 140	Aultbea to Inchnadamph 66.5 miles ascent 1312m	Gairloch to Ullapool 55 miles ascent 1078m	Aultbea to Ullapool 43 miles ascent 806m	Aultbea to Lael 34.5 miles ascent 730m
Lael — 160				
Ullapool				Lael to Inchnadamph 32 miles ascent 582m
— 180		Ullapool to Kylesku 60 miles ascent 1376m	Ullapool to Lochinver 35.5 miles ascent 606m	
Inchnadamph — 200				
Lochinver				Inchnadamph to Kylesku 36.5 miles ascent 870m
— 220	Inchnadamph to Rhiconich 57.5 miles ascent 1340m		Lochinver to Rhiconich 45.5 miles ascent 1240m	
Kylesku				
Scourie — 240		Kylesku to Tongue 64.5 miles ascent 1310m		Kylesku to Durness 35 miles ascent 714m
Rhiconich				
Durness — 260	Rhiconich to Melvich 69.5 miles ascent 1584m		Rhiconich to Tongue 43.5 miles ascent 840m	

Miles from Inverness	8 DAYS	10 DAYS	13 DAYS	17 DAYS
Durness ▶ — 260	Rhiconich to Melvich 69.5 miles ascent 1584m	Kylesku to Tongue 64.5 miles ascent 1310m	Rhiconich to Tongue 43.5 miles ascent 840m	Durness to Tongue 29.5 miles ascent 596m
— 280				
Tongue ▶ — 300		Tongue to Mey 56 miles ascent 1112m	Tongue to Thurso 43 miles ascent 979m	Tongue to Reay 32.5 miles ascent 822m
Bettyhill ▶				
Melvich ▶ — 320				
Reay ▶				Reay to John o'Groats 30.5 miles ascent 318m
Thurso ▶ — 340	Melvich to Melvich 73.5 miles ascent 828m		Thurso to Thurso 40.5 miles ascent 396m	
Mey ▶				
John o'Groats ▶ — 360		Mey to Melvich 43.5 miles ascent 460m		John o'Groats to Reay 31.5 miles ascent 354m
Thurso ▶ — 380				
Reay ▶			Thurso to Garvault 45 miles ascent 476m	Reay to Garvault 34 miles ascent 357m
Melvich ▶ — 400		Melvich to Altnaharra 48.5 miles ascent 445m		
Forsinard ▶	Melvich to Lairg 69 miles ascent 668m			
Garvaut ▶ — 420			Garvault to Lairg 40 miles ascent 389m	Garvault to Crask inn 27 miles ascent 342m
Altnaharra ▶ — 440		Altnaharra to Tain 46.5 miles ascent 299m		
Crask inn ▶				Crask Inn to Edderton 33.5 miles ascent 88m
Lairg ▶ — 460			Lairg to Cromarty 41 miles ascent 188m	
Edderton ▶ — 480	Lairg to Inverness 67 miles ascent 604m			Edderton to Cromarty 20.5 miles ascent 147m
Tain ▶				
Cromarty ▶ — 500		Tain to Inverness 41 miles ascent 528m	Cromarty to Inverness 26 miles ascent 416m	Cromarty to Inverness 26 miles ascent 416m
— 520				
Inverness ▶				

When forests like this in Strath Naver (Stage 13) are harvested, they are not being replanted

INTRODUCTION

An Teallach (1062m), the most impressive of the 27 Munro mountains en route (Stage 5)

Imagine hundreds of miles of unspoilt wilderness with a varied landscape of craggy mountains, verdant glens and rolling open peat moorland dotted with lochs (lakes) and lochans (smaller lakes) from which clear mountain streams feed into salmon- and trout-filled rivers. All this is surrounded by rugged coastlines where rocky cliffs are interspersed with sandy bays and deep sea inlets capable of sheltering ocean-going ships. Dotted across this wilderness are tiny communities, where a modern form of crofting (subsistence farming) flourishes, and a few small towns that provide the accoutrements of modern-day life. A filigree network of narrow roads and country lanes links these communities, enabling access to the mountains and lochs. But you do not need to imagine, for it all exists and can be found in the north Highlands of Scotland.

Separated from the rest of the country by the Great Glen, a deep gash formed by an ancient faultline, the human history of the north is one of isolation and independent living. Ancient tribes, such as the Picts who prevented Roman incursion and later Highland clans who fought brutally over the small areas of tillable land, maintained this separateness. It was not until governments in Edinburgh and London felt threatened by Jacobite rebellions, which originated in the Highlands, that action was taken to integrate the region with the rest of Britain. Military roads, bridges and fortifications were built, which opened up the country. A revolution in agriculture saw thousands of peasant crofters driven from the land as small-scale subsistence farming was replaced by large-scale sheep rearing. Many of the displaced crofters emigrated, others were resettled in planned coastal villages. Some found employment in a 19th-century herring fishing boom, which led to the construction of fishing ports around the coast with more new roads and eventually a railway to connect them to the south.

But despite improved communications and links with the outside world, the north of Scotland has remained a harsh place to live and many youngsters move away to find jobs. Over the years, various national and local government agencies, together with charitable foundations, have attempted to improve the living standards of the Highland population. In 2015 the latest of these, the North Highland Initiative, a body set up to integrate the promotion of business, tourism and agriculture, created the North Coast 500 (NC500). This is a circular route of just over 500 miles for tourists in cars, campervans and on motorcycles. Nicknamed 'Scotland's route 66', it has been very successful in showcasing what the north of Scotland has to offer and attracting motorised tourists from around the world to experience it first hand. Cyclists too have been attracted to ride the route, but many have been

The final Jacobite rebellion was defeated in 1746 at the Battle of Culloden near Inverness (Stage 1)

put off when they find that parts are on fast, potentially dangerous main roads and other parts are on very steep hills that are impassable for all but the super fit.

The cycle route around the north of Scotland described in this book seeks to address some of these problems. Like the signposted NC500, it starts and ends in the Highland regional capital, Inverness. However, instead of following busy main roads around the Beauly firth, it follows a quiet lane along the loch shore to pick up the signposted route at Muir of Ord. It then follows the NC500 right across Scotland to the west coast through the ancient county of Wester Ross.

Before turning up the coast, the motorist's NC500 circles the remote Applecross peninsula by climbing steeply over the Bealach na Bà pass, which with a gradient of up to 20 per cent is the steepest road in Scotland. You can follow this if you like (it is fully described as an alternative route), but for cyclists who want a less challenging ride this guide takes you directly to Shieldaig where the signposted NC500 route is rejoined.

This is followed for many miles, circling the west and north coasts through Sutherland and Caithness to reach Scotland's NE corner at John o' Groats. The return journey to Inverness signposted for motorists takes the NC500 down the busy A9 road, where fast cars and heavy freight traffic make for a nightmare ride. This guide takes an altogether different route that mostly follows the Far North Way, part of the National Cycle Network, along almost deserted lanes through the Sutherland flow country to Tain in Easter Ross. The final leg back to Inverness also avoids the A9 by following NCN1, also part of the National Cycle Network, which uses a local ferry across the mouth of the Cromarty firth then crosses the Black Isle before returning to Inverness, 528 miles since leaving the city.

En route it passes the foot of 27 Munros (Scottish mountains over 3000ft or 914m) and countless beaches, bays and sea lochs, where fish and seafood are caught to grace the menus of the many local hotels, inns and restaurants.

There are eight active whisky distilleries (plus one for gin) and five craft ale micro breweries, producing alcoholic beverages from barley grown on the Black Isle. The mountains and glens are home to large numbers of wild red deer and farmed Cheviot sheep, both of which also appear on menus as venison and lamb. Avian raptors, including golden eagles, cruise the sky above, while around the coast you can find grey seals, sea otters and bottlenose dolphins, with minke whales as seasonal visitors. The north coast route is already popular with motorised tourists. Now cyclists following the north of Scotland cycle route can discover for themselves why this iconic route has become one of the greatest coastal journeys in the world.

Cyclists passing Loch Naver (Stage 13)

BACKGROUND

For most of recorded history, life in the far north of Scotland has differed from that in the south, a variation that has its roots 2000 years ago when the Romans were in Britain. It is only since the coming of the railways in the 19th century that the region started to become more linked economically and socially with the rest of Scotland.

Pre-historic inhabitants (circa 8500BC–AD71)

Scotland became habitable after the last Ice Age ended circa 10,000BC. Successive waves of Stone Age, Bronze Age and Iron Age incomers, who probably arrived by sea, built settlements of basic turf, wood or stone houses mostly along the north and east coasts. Many of the best-preserved specimens are offshore on the Orkney islands, although some ruined brochs (circular defensive towers), stone circles and roundhouses can be found along the east coast (Stages 12A–14A). The best mainland example, on cliffs at Crosshill near Thurso (Stage 11), suffered from erosion and fell into the sea in 1972.

Romans and Picts (AD71–AD383)

The first references to Scotland appeared during Roman times. Having invaded southern England in AD43, Roman power spread north from AD71 when they reached southern Scotland and by AD84 had occupied the area south of the Highland Fault (a line running northeast from Loch Lomond to Montrose on the east coast). This presence proved to be temporary with the Romans withdrawing (AD122) into England and building a defensive

BACKGROUND

line (Hadrian's Wall) across the country between the Solway Firth and Tynemouth. While the Romans never reached the Highlands, their presence in central Scotland had an energising effect upon the disparate Iron Age tribes that inhabited the area, causing them to co-operate in resisting further Roman advances. This amalgam of Highland tribes became known by the Romans as the Picti (Picts) from the Latin *picta* (painted) as they decorated their bodies with dye.

Highland Picts and lowland Scots (AD383–circa AD900)

After the Romans left England, the Picts continued to dominate the Scottish Highlands, although with a decentralised structure of frequently warring clans. The west coast and Hebridean isles were settled by Gaels from Ireland as the Kingdom of Dál Riata.

Lowland Scotland was populated by tribes of ancient Britons pushed north by the Romans. They were joined by migrant Anglo-Saxons arriving from continental Europe via northern England who mixed with the local tribes and eventually coalesced to become known as the Scots. This split between the tribal north and a more cosmopolitan south was long lasting and continued to define Scottish society for many generations, being particularly evident during the 18th-century Jacobite rebellions. Irish missionaries brought Christianity to Scotland during the sixth and seventh centuries.

Vikings (AD793–1266)

Viking raiders from Scandinavia began attacking the coasts of Scotland and northern England in AD793. By the mid-ninth century their strategy changed from isolated raids into

Ruins of an Iron Age Pictish broch at Carn Liath (Stage 14A)

colonisation. While most of northern England was over run, Viking occupation of Scotland was confined to the western and northern isles and coastal areas of the north and west, including Caithness, Sutherland and parts of Ross. Resistance to Viking expansion is thought to be responsible for the ninth-century coming together of Picts, Gaels and Scots as the Kingdom of Alba which later became the Kingdom of Scotland. Viking settlement of mainland Scotland ended after the Battle of Largs (1263) and the subsequent treaty of Perth (1266), although they remained in control of the Orkney and Shetland isles until 1472.

Independent Kingdom of Scotland (AD900–1603)

From AD900, when Donald II was declared King of Alba, until the union of the Scottish and English crowns in 1603, Scotland was ruled by a succession of monarchs. At first threatened by Viking expansion then beset by frequent internal squabbles, by the late 13th century the main adversary was England. Independence wars against English invasions between 1296 and 1357 threw up famous resistance leaders William Wallace (who won the Battle of Stirling Bridge in 1297) and Robert the Bruce (victorious at Bannockburn 1314). Wallace's life was depicted in the 1995 film *Braveheart* while Bruce's victory has been eulogised by songwriter Roy Williamson of the Corries folk group in his 1966 song *Flower of Scotland*, which has become an unofficial Scottish anthem. One outcome of confrontations with England was the 'Auld Alliance', a mutual defence treaty between Scotland and France first signed in 1295 and renewed regularly until 1560. After further confrontations, which included a decisive English victory at Flodden (1513) and a period known as the Rough Wooing (1543–51) when the English tried to force unification by a marriage between Prince Edward (the heir to the throne) and Mary Queen of Scots, the 16th-century growth of Protestantism in Scotland and England eventually brought the countries closer together. In 1603 this alliance was formalised when the Protestant Stuart King James VI of Scotland inherited the English throne as James I.

Although part of Scotland, the underdeveloped and hard-to-reach north and west Highlands remained uninfluenced by national and international politics. The death of King Macbeth (1057) led to a gradual switch in Scotland from the tanist system of local governance (where clan leaders were chosen by consent – a system that caused frequent disputes) to a feudal system of primogeniture where succession as leader passed to the incumbent's oldest son. Loyalty in the north and west was to local clans who maintained the tanist system. Disputes between and within clans were common and cross clan-border raids frequent. A number of Scottish monarchs attempted to bring the lawless clans under central control, with little success. Although English became the lingua franca in lowland and eastern Scotland, Gaelic remained the language of the Highlands and Western isles.

Union with England and the Jacobites (1603–1746)

The union of the crowns in 1603 led eventually to a union of the countries. Near the end of the English Civil War (1642–51), Scotland's parliament declared for Charles II as the new king, rejecting Oliver Cromwell's claim to be Lord Protector (effectively a military dictator). Cromwell's army under General Monck invaded and occupied Scotland in 1650. A pro-Royalist rebellion in the north was put down by garrisoning a new fort in Inverness with 6000 English troops, one small tower of which remains (Stages 1 and 16). The glorious revolution (1688), when Stuart King James VII was overthrown as monarch and replaced with William of Orange, sparked renewed rebellion among Jacobite (pro-Stuart) clans in the north that intensified after the Act of Union (1707) created the United Kingdom of Great Britain and ended Scottish independent government.

Things came to a head in 1715 with the first Jacobite uprising in support of James Edward Stuart, the 'Old Pretender'. Although this was put down, a further rebellion in 1745, led by 'Bonnie Prince Charlie', James Edward Stuart's son, caused the government in London to take decisive measures, finally stamping out the Jacobite threat. Defeat of the mainly clan-based Jacobite army at Culloden near Inverness (1746) was followed by a hunting down and transportation or

Piles of stones that were once houses; all that remains of Grummore in Strath Naver, which was 'cleared' in 1814 (Stage 13)

killing of the rebels. Strict laws banned many of the practices of the Highland clans including the wearing of tartan or kilts and the carrying of weapons. Investment in military infrastructure including forts, roads and bridges made the Highlands easier to control. By these measures, clans were eventually transformed from aggressive tribal forces into benign social societies, while clan leaders no longer regarded clan members as human assets that could be called upon to fight for clan territory but rather as rent paying tenants who could provide landlords with an income.

Highland clearances (circa 1760–1855)

Following union with England, the lowland and eastern Scottish economy entered a period of rapidly growing prosperity. This was not experienced in the Highlands where over population, small farms and low surpluses of marketable output caused poverty among peasants and low rental income for landowners. The main products at the time were potatoes, barley and oats (all for local consumption) and black cattle, which were driven south for sale in the lowlands. Landowners discovered that they could increase the profitability of their estates by removing subsistence-farming peasants from their lands and replacing them with large sheep farms. The evicted tenants were often rehoused in small crofting settlements near the coast where kelp processing (seaweed burning to produce soda ash for use in soap and glass production) and fishing industries could enable

The monument at Helmsdale commemorates local crofters who emigrated during the great clearances (Stage 13A)

them to earn a small income to supplement their farming activity.

Some clearances were benign with evictees moving to a better lifestyle, while others were brutal with tenants being forcibly removed from their houses, which were then burnt while they watched. One of the most notorious practitioners of forced clearances was Patrick Sellar, the factor (property manager) for the largest estate in Scotland, that of the Duchess of Sutherland. He was the grandson of an evicted tenant who had moved out of the Highlands for a better life. Sellar attended Edinburgh university before returning to the Highlands convinced that clearances were, in the long run, in the tenants' best interests. He was responsible for the forced clearances in Strath Naver (Stage 13). In the later years of the clearances, forced evictions became less common with tenants often being offered financial incentives to emigrate. Many chose to migrate to Canada with an estimated 50,000 going to Nova Scotia. The Exiles memorial in Helmsdale (Stage 13A) commemorates this Highland diaspora.

Highland economy in the 19th and 20th centuries

While central Scotland became one of the powerhouses of the British empire, the inland Highland economy limped on. When the price of wool fell, some of the clearance sheep farms became sporting estates where a few prosperous southerners could stalk deer or fish for salmon. In coastal communities another kind of fish became an important part of the economy. Huge herring shoals migrate up the east coast of Britain every spring, reaching northern Scotland in the summer before returning south in the autumn. Exploitation of these shoals started in the 1780s when the British Fisheries Society began developing fishing boat harbours around the north Scottish coast. By 1880, thousands of boats were following the shoals at sea while thousands of women, many of them dispossessed crofters, made their way from port to port gutting, curing and packing the catch into barrels. The new far north railway carried the fish away for export, mostly to northern Germany and the Baltic states. The outbreak of World War I (1914) put an end to this trade and the 'herring boom' was over.

Nowadays the greatest quantity of fish processed in Scotland is salmon. While some of this is wild and caught at sea, and a very small amount line-caught from rivers, most is produced in salmon farms in west coast lochs. Two small west coast villages, Lochinver (Stage 6) and Kinlochbervie (off Stage 8), have become major fishing ports for deep-sea-caught white fish. Here European boats (mostly Spanish or French) land their catches for onward transport to the continent in refrigerated trucks.

During World War I, imports of timber from Europe were obstructed. This caused government concern and in 1919 the Forestry Commission was

Wick harbour housed the world's largest fishing fleet during the 19th-century herring boom (Stage 12A)

established with a remit to increase the supply of home-grown timber. A long-term plan to plant new forests commenced and the next 60 years saw a steady increase of forestry acreage, 70 per cent of which was in Scotland. This brought new plantations to the Highlands and a steady encroachment of trees on land previously used for sheep farming. In the 1960s, increased levels of income tax led high earners to search for ways to obtain tax relief with forestry investment proving to be very efficient. This led to large-scale private investment in new forests, which grew the acreage even more. However, most of these trees were fast-growing non-native conifers which brought criticism from environmentalists. The Forestry Commission now plants fewer trees and since tax relief was removed in 1988 there is less private investment. As mature plantations are harvested, many are not being replanted. In Forsinard (Stage 13), the Royal Society for the Protection of Birds (RSPB) has purchased a large area of cut-down forest intending to restore it as open moorland.

The first half of the 20th century saw a rapid increase in demand for electricity. In the south this was supplied by coal-fired power stations but in the Highlands the North of Scotland Hydro-Electric Board was established (1943) to construct power-generating dams throughout the area including a large dam at Lairg (Stage 14). The Highlands became an area for nuclear power research when Dounreay (Stage

Lairg dam and hydro-electric power station was completed in 1959 (Stage 14)

11) was opened in 1955. A test reactor was followed by a prototype fast-breeder reactor that supplied electricity to the grid. However, plans for a commercial power station were abandoned on cost grounds and the research site is being decommissioned.

The north Highlands have benefitted from the discovery of oil beneath the North Sea. Harbours at Inverness and Wick and around the Cromarty Firth all supply offshore drilling installations, while Wick airport is used to fly personnel to and from the rigs. Two huge construction yards were built to assemble drilling rigs at Kishorn (Stage 3) and Nigg (Stage 15) while Subsea 7 at Bridge of Wester (Stage 12A) is a 7 mile-long fabrication site for undersea pipelines. Inverness, Wick and Nigg harbours have become important centres for the construction and maintenance of off shore-electricity-generating wind turbines.

THE ROUTE

This guide describes a cycle-friendly touring route around Scotland's far north. Starting and finishing in the Highland capital Inverness, the circular route passes through the ancient counties of Wester Ross, Sutherland, Caithness, Easter Ross and Cromarty. The recommended route is 528 miles (850km) long, while a number of variants (some shorter, some longer) provide for a total distance varying between 475 and 555 miles (764 and 893km).

Stages 1 and 2 cross Scotland from east to west following quiet roads at first beside Beauly Firth then ascending very gently through the Black Water valley and Strath Bran before descending along Strath Carron to reach the west coast at Lochcarron. From here the main route turns north up the Atlantic coast (Stage 3), although a very challenging alternative (Stage 3A) can be followed that climbs over the Bealach na Bà pass (626m), the steepest and third-highest road in Scotland.

Continuing up the west coast, Stage 4 passes the dramatic Torridon mountains and undulates past Kinlochewe and Loch Maree before descending to Gairloch. Stage 5 circles the northern part of the Fisherfield peninsula then crosses a low pass over the shoulder of An Teallach and descends through Strath More to Ullapool, the first town since Inverness. On Stage 6 the main route enters the North West Highlands Geopark, turning inland onto a plateau of wild open land dotted with lochs and lochans before passing Ben More Assynt and returning to the coast at the small fishing port of Lochinver. An alternative route, which is closer to the coast, undulates past Stac Pollaidh across the southern part of the Assynt peninsula. Stages 7 and 8, which undulate frequently and sometimes steeply, first circle the Assynt peninsula then descend to go over Kylesku bridge and cross rocky open moorland before descending through the Dionard valley into Durness, close to the extreme northwest corner of Scotland.

Assynt has a landscape of rocky hills, deep sea lochs and tiny islands (Stage 7)

A seasonal ferry crosses the Cromarty Firth (Stage 15)

Stages 9–11 follow the rugged north coast from west to east, passing round a number of deep sea lochs and through Thurso to reach John o' Groats, famous as the most northerly village on the British mainland. From here, there are two ways to return south to Inverness. The main route (Stages 12–14) travels through the centre of the country following the Far North Way, part of the National Cycle Network route NCN1 on quiet minor roads through the Sutherland flow country, an area greatly affected by 19th-century land clearances. An alternative (Stages 12A–14A) uses the busy A9 main road along the east coast passing through Wick, Helmsdale, Brora and Dornoch before rejoining the main route at Tain. Between Tain and Inverness (Stages 15–16), a seasonal ferry (operates June–September) is used to cross a narrow straight at the entrance to Cromarty Firth before the route continues across the highly fertile Black Isle. An alternative route (Stages 15A–16A), for use when the ferry is not operating, passes through Dingwall, rejoining the main route before Inverness.

NATURAL ENVIRONMENT

Physical geography

The part of Scotland northwest of the Highland Boundary Fault has a complex geology built on a base of three-billion-year-old Lewisian gneiss, some of the oldest rocks in the world. These rocks were overlaid with Torridonian sandstones then uplifted during the Cambrian period to form mountains. About 430 million years ago, when the Laurentian and Baltic plates collided, part of these older rock strata were displaced laterally over the top of younger layers of red sandstone and limestone. Known as the Moine thrust and most clearly visible at Knockan crag (Stage 6), this thrust created a dividing line between higher jagged mountains to the west and lower, rounded hills in the east. The thrust line runs south from Loch Eriboll (Stage 9) on the north coast through Ben More Assynt (Stage 6) to Achnashellach in Strath Carron (Stage 2). Its identification by geologists John Horne and Ben Peach in 1884 led to the theory of plate tectonics, which explains the movement of the earth's crust. The geological significance of the region has been recognised by the establishment of the North West Highlands as a Geopark, a UNESCO designation for internationally important geological sites.

East of the thrust line, the Sutherland flow country (Stage 13) is a large expanse of low rolling hills covered with blanket peat bog. Near the coasts there are isolated terraces of limestone that provide fertile land around villages such as Durness (Stage 8) and Melvich (Stage 10). In the extreme northeast, Caithness is underlaid by beds of Devonian sandstone that have been extensively quarried to provide flagstones for street paving, particularly visible at Castletown (Stage 12).

In 1891, Sir Hugh Munro produced a list of all the mountains in Scotland that he believed to be over 3000ft (914m) in height. Modern measurement has refined the list and now there are 282 mountains classified as 'Munros'. 'Munro bagging' has become a modern-day phenomenon,

There are over 400,000 red deer in the Scottish Highlands

with thousands of walkers setting out every weekend to climb these mountains. There are 27 Munros with walking access points on or near the cycle route, mostly on the western section between Stages 2 and 6. These are listed in Appendix F. The highest of these, Sgùrr nan Clach Geala (1093m), is in the Fannich range south of Braemore junction (Stage 5).

Wildlife

The Scottish Highlands have a large population of red deer, with the stags most noticeable by the size of their antlers. They are extensively hunted, usually by stalking, during a season between July and October (for stags) and October and February (for hinds). Numbers have been increasing, with estimates of between 400,000 and 750,000 in Scotland. Unfortunately, these elegant animals have become something of a pest (they eat the shoots of young trees, damaging new plantations) and regular culls are organised to keep numbers down. There have even been suggestions

NATURAL ENVIRONMENT

of re-introducing wolves to control the deer population (wolves became extinct in Scotland at about the end of the 17th century), although this is being strongly resisted by local farmers who fear for their sheep. In addition, there are about 200,000 roe deer. Other land mammals that can be seen occasionally include mountain hares, badgers, red squirrels and pine martens. Very rare are Scottish wildcats.

Common sea mammals include grey seals and otters. Minke whales can be seen off the north and west coasts while bottlenose dolphins have made their home along the east coast, particularly around the Moray Firth where there is a pod of about 150 animals. Good viewing points are at Kessock bridge near Inverness (Stages 1 and 16) and Cromarty (Stage 16) where daily boat trips go out to see dolphins at close hand.

Salmon come in two kinds. Wild Atlantic salmon hatch in Highland rivers, swim out to sea for three or four years then return to their home river to breed and die. In late summer, mature salmon can often be seen leaping up the waterfalls at Rogie (Stage 1) or Shin (Stage 14) on their way to spawn. Much more numerous are farmed salmon raised in pens in sheltered west coast inlets and lochs. Rope-grown mussels are another major aquacultural product, while trout farms can be found in inland glens.

Although not strictly wildlife, cattle and sheep are an important part of the Scottish Highland scene. Traditionally, crofters raised one or two black cows as a commercial crop, which were sold to itinerant drovers

Atlantic salmon jumping the Falls of Shin on their way to spawn upriver (Stage 14)

who collected cattle from many farms. The animals were driven south, first to markets in Crieff or Falkirk then on to England (during the 18th century, 80 per cent of beef consumed in London arrived on the hoof from Scotland). Modern-day Highland cattle, with large horns and long, shaggy, mostly brown coats, are direct descendants of the old black cattle. The farms of Caithness in the far north nowadays raise herds of black Aberdeen Angus beef cattle for the English market, but these are butchered in Scotland and transported south in refrigerated vehicles. The clearances brought large flocks of Cheviot and blackface sheep (selected for their ability to withstand the harsh climate) to the north Highlands, and they remain the dominant breeds today. After fattening on the hills, many of the lambs are sold in August through Lairg market (Stage 14) where sales of 15,000 lambs make this the biggest sheep market in Europe.

The iconic golden eagle is Scotland's most famous bird of prey, but there are other raptors to be

Highland cattle and Cheviot sheep are reared throughout the north Highlands

A small remnant of the Caledonian pine forest on an island in Loch Assynt (Stage 6)

seen too. Most populations were in decline, but conservation efforts and re-introductions since the 1960s have led to increasing numbers of buzzards, hen harriers, red kites (on Black Isle, Stage 16), sparrow hawks and peregrine falcons in the northern Highlands. At Forsinard (Stage 13), the RSPB has created a large bird sanctuary in the blanket peat bog of the Sutherland flow country. Many birds are seen, including dippers, dunlins, plovers and greenshanks.

Flora

Following the end of the last Ice Age, most of Britain became covered in large forests dominated by Scots pine and birch. As the climate warmed, Scots pines, which thrive on rocky terrain, peaty areas or poor sandy soils, died off in the south, but remained predominant in the cooler region of northern Scotland as part of the Caledonian forest. The last 3000 years has seen a steady decline in ancient forest due to human activities such as use of wood for construction, burning as fuel or clearing land for sheep farming. Only small remnants of ancient forest remain, usually in remote areas where the soil is too rocky or too poor for anything else to grow. Since 1918 government policy has been to encourage tree planting, mostly in large commercial forests of Sitka spruce, Douglas fir and larch. Nowadays, as these forests mature and are harvested, they are being replaced with native broadwood trees (oak and birch) and Scots pine to provide a more natural environment.

PREPARATION

When to go?
The route is best followed between April and October when the days are longer, the weather is milder and there is little chance of snow. Accommodation is in heavy demand in July and August and if you travel at this time, advance booking is essential even for hostels.

How long will it take?
The route has been broken into 16 stages averaging 33 miles (53km) per stage. A fit cyclist, cycling an average of 53 miles (85km) per day, should be able to complete the ride in 10 days. A more leisurely daily ride of 40 miles (64km) would see the ride accomplished in 13 days. There are a variety of places to stay overnight, making it possible to tailor daily distances to your requirements. A selection of alternative schedules is shown at the beginning of this guide.

What kind of cycle is suitable?
As the route is almost entirely on asphalt surfaced roads almost any type of cycle can be used, although touring bikes and hybrids are the most suitable. Racing bikes can be used, provided they can carry your luggage and have gearing suitable for steep climbs. There is no advantage in using a mountain bike (other than its low gearing for climbs) and if you do use one, you should replace the knobbly tyres with road tyres. Front suspension is beneficial as it absorbs much of the vibration. Straight handlebars with bar-ends enable you to vary your position regularly. Make sure your cycle is serviced and lubricated before you start, particularly the brakes, gears and chain.

As important as the bike is your choice of tyres. Slick road tyres are less suitable and knobbly mountain bike tyres not necessary. What you need is something inbetween with good tread and a slightly wider profile than you would use for everyday cycling at home. To reduce the chance of punctures, choose tyres with puncture-resistant armouring, such as a Kevlar™ band.

Cycle hire
If you cannot transport your own bike to Scotland, Ticket to Ride in Inverness has a wide range of hybrid, touring, mountain and electric bikes for hire. They operate from the pavilion in Bellfield Park, a 15min walk south from the centre of Inverness (www.tickettoridehighlands.co.uk). If you do hire a bike, you will often be more comfortable if you bring your own tried-and-trusted saddle and safety helmet. For contact details see Appendix E.

GETTING THERE AND BACK

Getting to and from the start
The start of the route outside Inverness castle is a short ride from Inverness

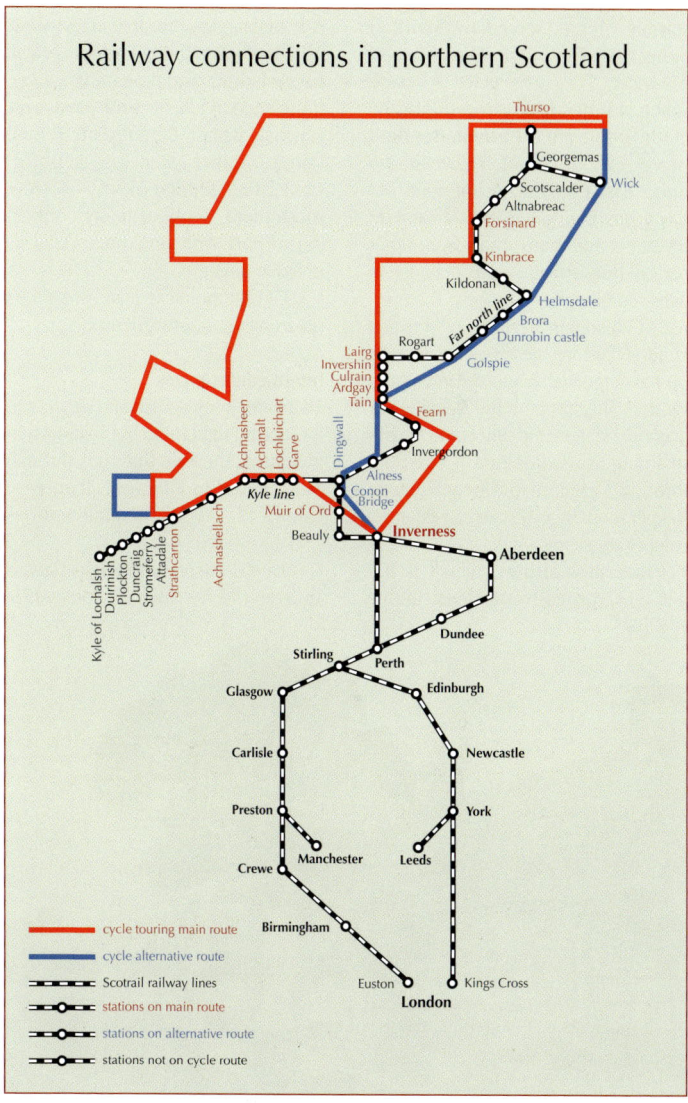

station. This is served by **ScotRail** trains from Edinburgh, Glasgow and Aberdeen that carry cycles. As cycle space is limited, booking should be made in advance through ScotRail (www.scotrail.co.uk). There is one direct **East Coast main line** train per day from London (King's Cross) to Inverness and many trains from other parts of Britain that require a change in either Edinburgh or Glasgow. The overnight **Caledonian Sleeper** runs between London (Euston) and Inverness, picking up passengers at Watford, Crewe and Preston. This has both full sleeping-car accommodation and one carriage with reclining seats. Booking is essential through Caledonian Sleeper (www.sleeper.scot). Bicycles are carried at no extra charge.

Inverness airport, which is 8.5 miles (13.5km) east of the city beside the A96, is served by British Airways (www.britishairways.com), EasyJet (www.easyjet.com) and Loganair (www.loganair.co.uk) flights from Heathrow, Gatwick, Belfast, Birmingham, Bristol, Luton, Manchester and Dublin. KLM (www.klm.co.uk) fly in from Amsterdam. ScotRail trains connect the airport with Inverness (17/day, irregular timing).

Getting home is just a matter of reversing your outward journey.

Intermediate access

There are two ScotRail train services in the north Highlands, both starting in Inverness. The **Kyle line** runs through Muir of Ord to Dingwall, then west calling at a series of small stations

Forsinard is one of many remote stations served by the Far North line (Stage 13)

along Stage 2 between Garve and Strathcarron. The **Far North line** runs from Dingwall to Wick and Thurso, calling at stations on the east coast and up through the centre of Scotland. Principal stations are Alness, Tain, Lairg, Golspie, Brora and Helmsdale with many small stations in-between. There are four trains per day on each route (Monday–Saturday), although only one on Sundays. All these services carry cycles, however, space is limited. There are no stations on Stages 3–10.

The Durness Bus company (www.thedurnessbus.com) operates a number of scheduled routes using minibuses liveried as The **Far North Bus**, with cycle carrying facilities. Connecting the north and south of the region, route 805 links Inverness with Durness via Lairg four days/week, while route 806 runs daily between Lairg and Durness. Along the north coast, route 803 runs between Durness and Thurso on Saturdays only, with additional journeys on Tuesdays and Thursdays from Tongue to Thurso. On the northwest coast, route 804 goes from Kinlochbervie to Lochinver on Tuesdays and Thursdays. Bicycle spaces must be reserved at least 24hr in advance by phoning or texting 0778 211 0007.

Ticket to Ride in Inverness (www.tickettoridehighlands.co.uk/cyclist-transport tel 01463 419160) operates a cycle-carrying mini-bus on routes Inverness–John o' Groats and Inverness–Garve–Ullapool–Lochinver–Durness. These are not scheduled services but operate on demand like a shared taxi. The price for two passengers with bikes from Inverness to John o' Groats or Durness is £350 (£175 each); for six passengers it is £490 (£82 each). From Inverness to Ullapool the price for two is £190 (£95 each) and £270 (£45 each) for six. They try to match up passengers and dates with available spaces are posted on their website.

NAVIGATION AND INFORMATION

Waymarking

The NC500 route, which forms the basis for Stages 1–11 and 12A–16A, has been signposted by Transport Scotland and is shown on official road signs at all significant road junctions.

Most of the route through the centre of northern Scotland (Stages 12–16) is part of the Sustrans National Cycle Network (NCN). Between John o' Groats and Tain (Stages 12 and 14) this is waymarked as 'Far North Way', while between Tain and Inverness (Stages 15–16) it is waymarked NCN1.

Maps

The best map of the motorists' route is Nicholson North Coast Journey (1:150,000) (ISBN 98781912046652), which is a series of strip maps at a scale suitable for cyclists. However, this does not cover the inland Stages 13 and 14.

CYCLING THE NORTH COAST 500

Waymarks and signposts en route, clockwise from top left: NC500 waymark, NC500 road sign used by Transport Scotland, Far North Way sign, National Cycle Network route 1 sign

OS Road map of Northern Scotland (1:250,000) (ISBN 9780139263730) covers the whole route. OS Landranger maps (1:50,000) give more detailed coverage, probably more detail than you need for a long-distance cycle ride, and 13 sheets are needed to cover the entire route. However, if used in conjunction with the Nicholson map, only four sheets are needed for the inland areas not covered by Nicholson.
- 10 Strath Naver
- 16 Lairg & Loch Shin
- 17 Helmsdale & Strath of Kildonan
- 21 Dornoch & Alness

Various online maps are available to download, at a scale of your choice. Particularly useful is Open Street Map (www.openstreetmap.org), which has an option showing British NCN cycle routes including NCN1. The website of the commercial organisation that runs NC500 has an interactive map of their route at www.northcoast500.com.

Guidebooks
Photographer Charles Tait has self-published *The North Coast 500 Guide Book* (ISBN 9781909036604). This is aimed primarily at motorised tourists with little regard for the needs of cyclists. Rough guides publish *The Rough Guide to the North Coast 500* (ISBN 9781789194074). While not a guidebook, David M Addison's *Exploring the NC500, Travelling Scotland's Route 66* (ISBN 9780993403249) is a very readable description of many of the places, and some of the history, to be found along the route.

NAVIGATION AND INFORMATION

Collins publishes two NC500 guides. *North Coast 500, Where to Eat and Stay* (ISBN 9780008547066) is a comprehensive guide to restaurants, cafés, hotels, B&Bs, hostels and campsites en route, while *North Coast 500, Britain's ultimate road trip* is a glossy large format-book with stunning pictures.

There are lots of general guidebooks to the Scottish Highlands including some specifically aimed at cyclists. In addition, there are specialist books giving climbing details for Munros and others that list and provide tasting notes for whisky distilleries. Most of these maps and guidebooks are available from leading bookshops including Stanford's, London and The Map Shop, Upton upon Severn. Relevant maps are widely available en route.

Tourist information

The Scottish national tourist board, now known as VisitScotland, which used to operate local tourist information offices throughout Scotland, has changed its strategy in recent years. Recognising the growth of online information and booking, most information offices in the far north have been closed. The two remaining centres in Inverness (Stages 1/16) and Ullapool (Stage 5) have been renamed as iCentres. In addition, there is one commercial tourist information office in John o' Groats (Stage 10) and one locally run tourist office in Gairloch (Stage 4). VisitScotland has set up an online information service based upon 14 local hubs that can be accessed via their main site (www.visitscotland.com/destinations-maps/highlands/).

The remote youth hostel at Achmelvich beach in Assynt (Stage 7)

Local councils and community groups have been encouraged to set up their own tourist websites and these are listed in Appendix B.

ACCOMMODATION

Hotels, guesthouses and bed & breakfast

For most of the route there is a wide variety of accommodation although the number of establishments varies greatly from stage to stage. The stage descriptions identify all places known to have accommodation at the time of publication. Hotels vary from expensive five-star properties to modest local establishments and most usually offer a full meal service. Guesthouses and B&B accommodation generally offer only breakfast. Most places can be directly reserved online or via booking engines. The motorists' route is popular and it may be difficult to find places with vacancies in July and August, making it prudent to book well in advance. Most properties are cycle friendly and will find you a secure overnight place for your pride and joy.

Youth hostels and bunkhouses

There are six official and two associated Scottish Youth Hostel Association (SYHA) hostels en route, one in Inverness (Stages 1 and 16) and seven spread along the west coast (Stages 4–8). SYHA is affiliated to Hostelling International and discounts are offered to members of other affiliated associations including the YHA in England. In addition, there are six private backpackers' hostels in Inverness and another 16 private hostels and bunkhouses spread along the route.

All of these properties are listed in Appendix C. Some provide sheets and blankets, but not all, and if planning to use these facilities it is best to arrive with a sleeping bag. Youth hostels, private hostels and bunkhouses have self-catering kitchens where guests can prepare their own food. Larger youth hostels (such as Inverness) provide meals, as do bunkhouses that are associated with neighbouring hotels or cafés such as Ledgowan Lodge (Stage 2), Kinlochewe (Stage 4) or An Cala café (Stage 6).

Camping

If you are prepared to carry camping equipment, this will probably be the cheapest way of cycling the route. Campsites on or near the route are listed in Appendix D. Camping may be possible in other locations with the permission of local landowners. A problem to be aware of when camping is midges. These tiny flying insects proliferate in the Highlands during early summer and are particularly active in the evenings. Repellent and even a mosquito head net are essential to keep them at bay.

Typical Scottish meal of haggis, neeps and tatties, with cranachan for dessert

FOOD AND DRINK

Where to eat
There are many places where cyclists can eat and drink, varying from cafés and tea-rooms through fish and chip shops to pubs, inns and upmarket restaurants. Locations of eateries are listed in stage descriptions, but these are not exhaustive. The only fast food outlets are in Inverness.

When to eat
Breakfast in Scottish hotels, guest-houses and B&Bs (normally included in the cost of overnight accommodation) is usually a cooked meal comprising porridge (oatmeal cooked with water and a little salt) followed by a 'full Scottish' (eggs, bacon, sausage, tomato, black pudding) served with toast and washed down with tea. Enough to set you up for the day! If you are cycling, you will probably prefer a light snack for lunch followed by a larger meal in the evening. Most cafés, pubs and restaurants can provide both.

What to eat
For many years, Scotland was known neither for the standard nor variety of its cuisine. Since the 1960s Scottish catering has greatly improved and is now on par with most other European countries. While restaurants and cafés serve a wide variety of British and international dishes, there are a number of local dishes you may like to try. Soup as a starter is a staple part

of Scottish dining. Tomato, lentil and vegetable soups are the most common but Scotch broth (mutton, pearl barley and vegetable) and Cullen skink (smoked haddock, potato, onion and cream) are particularly Scottish. Local beef, lamb and pork all feature as main courses, as does venison (deer). Scotland's most well-known dish is haggis, a traditional item made from a sheep's stomach stuffed with minced lung and oatmeal although nowadays artificial casings have replaced the stomach. Haggis can be served in a number of ways but the most common is with neeps and tatties (swede and potatoes). Scotch pies are a snack item made from cheap cuts of fatty mutton.

Unsurprisingly for a country surrounded on three sides by water, there is a wide variety of fish and seafood on menus. Salmon and trout, either wild, farmed or smoked are popular, while cod, haddock and sea bass are the most common white fish. Although not as common as in the days of the herring boom, herring can be found either as a main meal fried in oatmeal or smoked as kippers and served for breakfast. Mussels and scallops on menus are usually obtained locally.

Cranachan (raspberries blended in a mixture of cream, oatmeal, honey and whisky) is the most iconic Scottish dessert while clootie dumpling (steamed suet pudding made with dried fruits and spices) served with custard is a very filling alternative.

What to drink

Scotland is a beer-consuming country, with lager and heavy (the Scottish name for bitter or ale) the two most

The Black Isle Brewery produces a range of organic craft beers (Stage 16)

A dram from each of the whisky and gin distilleries passed would give you quite a hangover

popular forms. Tennent's is the leading lager while Deuchars and Belhaven are the best-selling ales. In recent years there has been an explosion of sales of traditionally produced craft ales, both on draught and in bottles. These are mostly produced by small local brewers including Strathcarron Brewery (Stage 2), An Tellach Ale (Stage 5), John o' Groats Brewery (Stage 11/12), Cromarty Brewing and Black Isle Brewery (both Stage 16), which are on or near the route. The latter also owns a real ale pub and hostel in the centre of Inverness.

The drink most associated with Scotland is Scotch whisky, a strong spirit made from water, fermented barley and yeast that typically contains between 40 and 43 per cent alcohol and must have been matured in cask for at least three years, but often much longer. Scotch, which accounts for 20 per cent of all British food and drink exports, is produced in 128 distilleries spread across the country, mostly using traditional techniques and strictly regulated production methods. Blended whisky is made by combining the output of various distilleries to produce an unchanging taste. Popular brands such as Famous Grouse, Bells and Johnnie Walker are all blended whiskies. The Scots usually consume blended whisky diluted with water. Single malt whiskies are the output of a single distillery and usually carry the name of that distillery such as Glenmorangie (Stage 15). They tend to be more expensive than blends. Whisky distilleries are classified into five kinds by their location: highland, Speyside, Islay, Campbeltown and lowland. The eight active distilleries passed on the cycle route are all highland distilleries with some producing single malts and others producing whisky for blending. They are listed in Appendix G and many can be visited.

All the usual soft drinks (colas, lemonade, fruit juices, mineral waters) are widely available. Irn Bru, a local fizzy drink produced in Glasgow to a 'secret' recipe, is the biggest selling non-alcoholic drink in Scotland.

AMENITIES AND SERVICES

Grocery shops
Most of the villages passed through have a small grocery store while the larger towns (Ullapool, Thurso, Wick, Golspie, Tain and Dingwall) have supermarkets and pharmacies.

Cycle shops
There are a number of cycle shops with repair facilities in Inverness and others spread randomly along the route, although there are often long distances between them. Some provide a call out repair service. Cycle shops are listed in Appendix E.

Currency and banks
Scotland, together with the rest of Britain, uses the pound sterling. Scottish currency notes circulate in parallel with Bank of England notes and both are legal tender. Many rural banks have closed and been replaced with mobile branches that visit one day per week – not much use for tourists. The remaining banks, all with ATM machines, are in Inverness, Gairloch, Ullapool, Thurso, Wick, Golspie, Tain, Alness and Dingwall, however, very few offer over-the-counter currency exchange. In addition, there are ATM machines in some post offices, garages and supermarkets. Travellers' cheques are rarely used.

Telephone and internet
Most of the route has mobile phone coverage, but in some remote locations the signal may be poor. The international dialling code for the UK is +44. Almost all hotels, guesthouses and hostels and many restaurants make internet access available to guests, usually free.

Beside Little Loch Broom (Stage 5)

Electricity
Voltage is 220v, 50HzAC. Plugs in Britain are three-pin square. Adapters can be purchased to convert both European and American plugs to the UK standard.

WHAT TO TAKE

Clothing and personal items
Although there is only one major climb (over the Bealach na Bà as an alternative route on Stage 3) the route undulates steeply and frequently, and as a consequence weight should be kept to a minimum. You will need clothes for cycling (shoes, socks, shorts/trousers, shirt, fleece, waterproofs) and clothes for evenings and days off. The best maxim is two of each, 'one to wear, one to wash'. Time of year makes a difference as you need more and warmer clothing in April/May and September/October. All of this clothing should be able to be washed en route, and a small tube or bottle of travel wash is useful. A sun hat and sunglasses are essential, while gloves and a woolly hat are advisable except in high summer.

In addition to your usual toiletries you will need sun cream and lip salve. You should take a simple first-aid kit. If staying in hostels you will need a towel and torch (your cycle light should suffice). During the summer, midges are a problem throughout the Highlands. A strong deet-based repellent will help keep them at bay.

Cycle equipment
Everything you take needs to be carried on your cycle. If overnighting in accommodation, a pair of rear panniers or a large seatpack should be sufficient to carry all your clothing and equipment, but if camping, you may also need front panniers. Panniers should be 100 per cent watertight. If in doubt, pack everything inside a strong polythene lining bag. Rubble bags, obtainable from builders' merchants, are ideal for this purpose. A bar-bag is a useful way of carrying items you need to access quickly such as maps, sunglasses, camera, spare tubes, puncture repair kit and tools. A transparent map case attached to the top of your bar-bag is an ideal way of displaying maps and guidebooks.

Your cycle should be fitted with mudguards and bell, and be capable of carrying water bottles, pump and lights. Many cyclists fit an odometer to measure distances. A basic toolkit should consist of puncture repair kit, spanners, Allen keys, adjustable spanner, screwdriver, spoke key and chain repair tool. Some cyclists carry a small roll of duct tape, useful for temporary repairs to bike or clothing. The only essential spares are two spare tubes. On a long cycle ride your chain will need regular lubrication and you should either carry a can of spray-lube or make regular visits to cycle shops. A strong lock is advisable.

SAFETY AND EMERGENCIES

Weather
Scotland is in the cool temperate zone with mild summers, cool winters and year-round moderate rainfall. Daily weather patterns are highly variable, it can be dreich (damp and drizzling) one moment and bright warm sunshine the next. In northern Scotland winds can blow from any direction but the most common is from the west/southwest/northwest. Such winds would give a headwind on Stages 1, 2 and 12.The weather is an important consideration when planning daily cycling distances.

Road safety
Most of the route is on quiet main roads with light traffic. However, many of these roads are single lane with passing places usually about 200 metres apart. This poses a serious problem for cyclists, particularly when cycling uphill. You will need to pull over both to let oncoming traffic past and allow following traffic to overtake. On the long climb over the Bealach na Bá (Stage 3A) or on the narrow undulating roads of the Assynt peninsula (Stage 7) this can become a very tedious procedure. In poor weather, visibility can often be limited. In order to ensure motorists see you, it is essential to have good lights and wear a high-vis fluorescent jacket. Scotland does not require compulsory wearing of cycle helmets, but their use is recommended.

The coastal NC500 route has become very popular with motorised tourists, including many with campervans and motorbikes. Campervan drivers are usually very considerate, but the width of their vehicles can be a problem for cyclists on narrow roads. Motorcyclists pose a greater

Average temperature (max/min °C)

	Apr	May	Jun	Jul	Aug	Sept	Oct
Inverness	12/4	15/6	17/9	19/11	19/11	16/9	13/6
Ullapool	11/5	14/7	16/9	17/11	17/11	15/10	13/8
Thurso	10/4	12/5	14/8	16/10	16/10	14/9	12/6

Average rainfall (mm/rainy days)

	Apr	May	Jun	Jul	Aug	Sept	Oct
Inverness	39/9	52/11	59/11	53/10	60/12	67/12	78/13
Ullapool	75/14	71/13	77/14	75/15	97/16	141/18	165/22
Thurso	50/12	49/11	53/10	62/12	65/13	74/14	95/17

Many of the roads are single track with passing places, like this on Stage 8

threat. Most ride sensibly and will give you consideration as they pass. However, a small minority ride as if they were TT racers making them a danger both to themselves and other road users.

From John o' Groats to Tain (Stages 12A–14A), the motorists' route mostly follows the A9, a busy road that has been widened and straightened with a resultant increase in traffic speed. Unless you are experienced in riding on busy roads with fast traffic you should follow the recommended inland route along quiet country roads, described in Stages 12–14.

Emergencies
In the unlikely event of an accident, the standardised emergency phone number is 112. The entire route has mobile phone coverage. Provided you have an EHIC card issued by your home country, medical costs of EU citizens are covered under reciprocal health insurance agreements.

Theft
In general, the route is safe and the risk of theft low. However, you should always lock your cycle and watch your belongings.

Insurance
Travel insurance policies usually cover you when cycle touring but they do not normally cover damage to, or theft of, your bicycle. If you have a household contents policy, this may cover cycle theft, but limits may be less than the actual cost of your cycle. Cycling UK, previously known as the Cyclists' Touring Club (CTC), offer a policy tailored to the needs of cycle tourists: www.cyclinguk.org.uk.

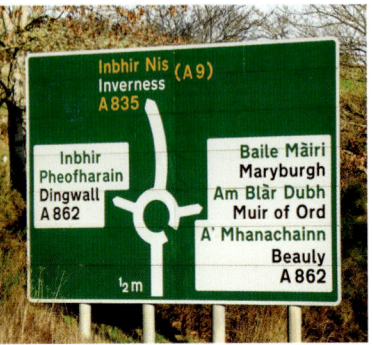

Gaelic appears on road signs like this one on Stage 1

ABOUT THIS GUIDE

Text and maps
There are 22 stages (16 on the main route, six on alternative routes) each covered by separate maps drawn to a scale of 1:150,000. Maps of the six urban areas (Inverness, Ullapool, Thurso, Wick, Tain and Dingwall) are drawn to a scale of 1:40,000. The main route line is shown in red with alternative routes in blue.

Places mentioned in the text are shown in **bold** if they appear on the maps. The abbreviation 'sp' in the text indicates a signpost. Distances shown are cumulative miles within each stage. For each city/town/village passed an indication is given of facilities available (accommodation, hostel, refreshments, camping, tourist office, cycle shop, station) when the guide was written. This list is neither exhaustive nor does it guarantee that establishments are still in business. No attempt has been made to list all such facilities as this would require another book the same size as this one. Appendix A summarises the facilities included in the stage descriptions.

GPX tracks
GPX tracks for the routes in this guidebook are available to download free at www.cicerone.co.uk/1219/gpx. A GPS device is an excellent aid to navigation, but you should also carry a map and compass and know how to use them. GPX files are provided in good faith, but neither the author nor the publisher accepts responsibility for their accuracy.

Language
Since the failed 18th-century Jacobite rebellions there has been a steady decline in the use of Gaelic which is nowadays spoken by less than two per cent of the Scottish population. English is the lingua franca of Scotland, although in the Highlands and Islands there is a cultural movement to revive Gaelic. It now appears on road signs, railway timetables and other official notices, but you will seldom hear it spoken. The most common use of the language is for geographic features (mountains, lakes, etc) that have retained their Gaelic names.

THE ROUTE

Cyclist on the Assynt peninsula (Stage 7)

STAGE 1
Inverness to Garve

Start	Inverness castle (24m)
Finish	Garve hotel (72m)
Distance	24.5 miles (39.5km)
Ascent	237m
Descent	189m
Waymarking	NCN1 Inverness to North Kessock then cycle route 20 to Muir of Ord and NC500 to Garve

The motorists' route follows a busy main road south of Beauly Firth to reach Muir of Ord. The cycle route described here avoids this road by leaving Inverness on Kessock bridge over the firth and following quiet side roads along the north shore. After Muir of Ord the motorists' NC500 route is joined following the Black Water river through a forested gorge to the village of Garve which sits beneath the bulk of Ben Wyvis. The stage is mostly flat with a gentle climb towards the end.

INVERNESS

Known as the 'Highland capital', Inverness (pop 63,750) (accommodation, hostel, refreshments, camping, tourist office, cycle shop, station) is the commercial and administrative centre for the Highland region of Scotland and one of the fastest growing cities in Europe. A settlement developed from the sixth century at a strategically important point where the Great Glen reaches the Moray Firth beside the easiest crossing point of the river Ness and it was here that Saint Columba is said to have converted the King of the Picts to Christianity. A castle was built in 1057 by King Malcolm III after his defeat of Macbeth and was the home to a number of early Scottish kings. Inverness, as the town beneath the castle became known, became a royal burgh in the 12th century. The castle was involved in various Scottish power struggles including capture by Robert the Bruce (1307), Mary Queen of Scots (1562) and Bonnie Prince Charlie (1746). When, later the same year, the Prince's

STAGE 1 – INVERNESS TO GARVE

Cromwell's tower in Inverness is all that remains of a 17th-century fort that housed 6000 soldiers

Jacobite rebels were crushed by the Hanoverians at Culloden just outside Inverness, the castle was blown up and left in ruins. The structure seen today dates from 1836 when a new red sandstone castle was built in neo-Norman Scottish baronial style. It was built to hold the Sheriff court, county hall and a gaol and has never functioned as a castle. The court has moved out and the building is closed during renovations. It is due to reopen in 2025.

In addition to the castle, Inverness has an unfinished Episcopal cathedral (1869) with two truncated towers that should have been topped with spires. Cromwell's tower, a small clocktower by the harbour, is all that remains of a large fort built by Oliver Cromwell to hold 6000 soldiers. The Victorian covered market was built in 1890 after a fire destroyed an earlier building. There are three road bridges, two pedestrian bridges and a railway bridge over the Ness. Downstream of the city, Kessock bridge was built in 1982 to link Inverness across the Beauly Firth with the Black Isle. The low-lying land between the city and the bridge has been developed as a thriving industrial estate.

From E side of Inverness castle follow track N, descending ramp towards city centre. After carrying your cycle down short flight of steps at bottom of ramp, continue ahead (Castle Wynd) past city museum and art gallery L to reach main road. ▶ Turn L (Bridge St), then after 100 metres turn R at traffic lights (Bank St) beside river Ness.

Do not worry, the steps are not a foretaste of what is to come. The only other steps are over a bridge at Invershin in Stage 14.

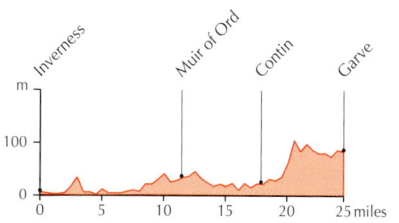

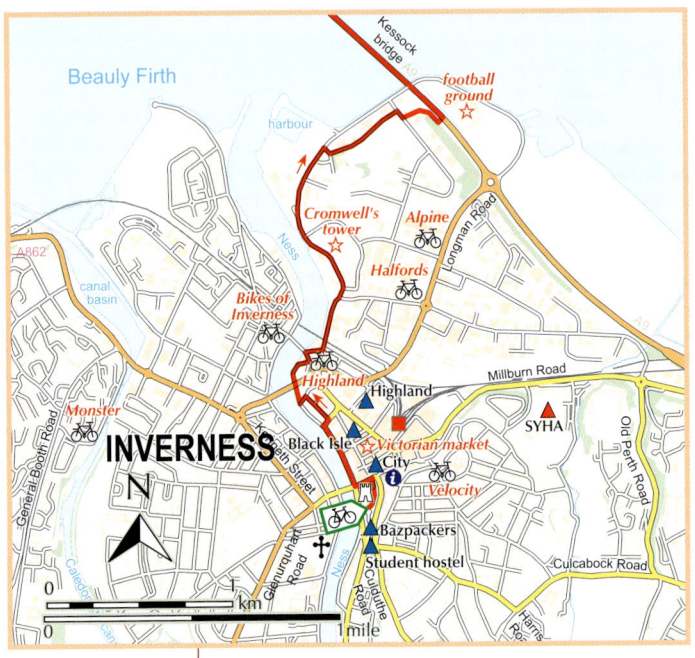

Pass Greig St pedestrian suspension bridge L and where road ahead becomes one-way street, follow road bearing R (Friars Lane). Turn first L (Friars St) beside telephone exchange and at end turn L (Glebe St). Turn R on cycle track beside river, passing under road bridge. Continue into Riverside St and follow this bearing R away from river to reach T-junction. Turn L (Waterloo Pl), then sharply R (Portland Pl) before river bridge. Go ahead through bollards and turn L (Shore St), passing under railway bridge. Continue between river L and industrial area R and go ahead over mini-roundabout. Road becomes Cromwell Rd, passing through industrial estate. ◄ Continue ahead on Longman Dr past entrance to harbour L, then turn second R and immediately L (still called Longman Dr). At T-junction, turn R and after 50 metres L onto asphalt cycle track. At end turn sharply L on cycle track beside A9 main

Red sandstone clocktower R (known as Cromwell's tower) stands on the site of a fort ordered to be constructed by Oliver Cromwell.

STAGE 1 – INVERNESS TO GARVE

Kessock bridge over Beauly Firth connects Inverness with the Black Isle

road and follow this over Kessock bridge crossing Beauly Firth. ▶ On other side of bridge, fork L through bollards and follow Old Craigton Rd downhill. Bear R alongside firth on Main St through **North Kessock** (3.5 miles, 4m) (accommodation, refreshments).

Where road bears R away from firth, turn L (sp Charleston) through **Charleston** and continue beside

Kessock was one of three bridges built in the 1980s across coastal firths that opened up road links with the northern Highlands (the others were over the Cromarty and Dornoch firths).

Glen Ord distillery in Muir of Ord produces The Singleton malt whisky for export and blending whisky for Johnnie Walker

CYCLING THE NORTH COAST 500

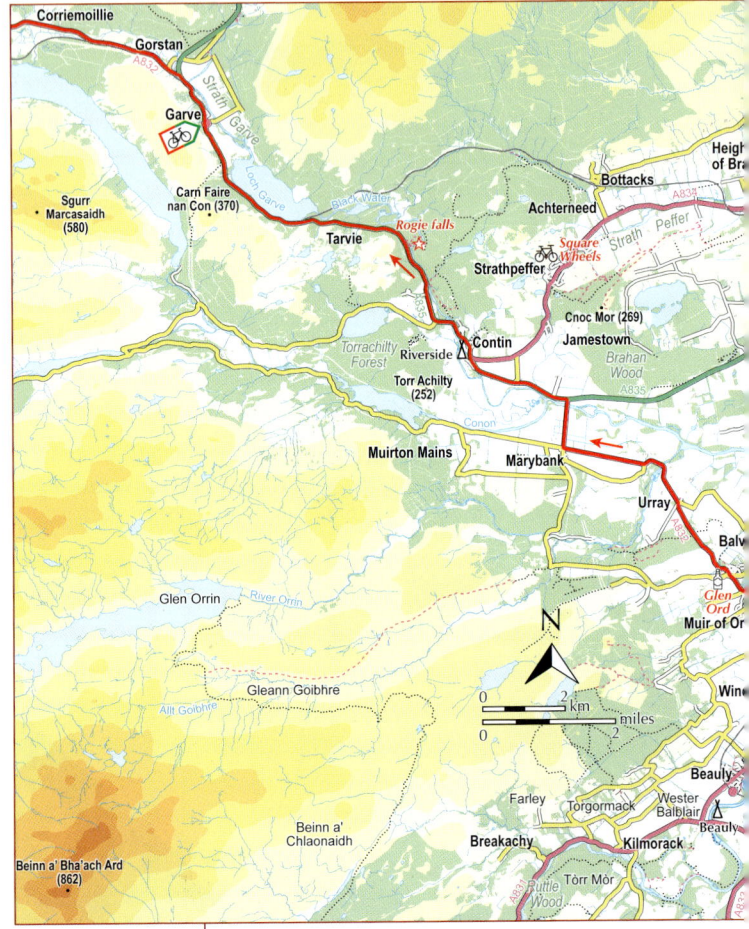

firth on quiet road past Coulmore bay caravan park. At **Redcastle** follow road bearing R uphill, away from firth, then 100 metres beyond hamlet turn L and continue to reach main road at Garguston. Turn L (A832, sp Muir of Ord) and follow main road to **Muir of Ord** (12 miles, 35m)

STAGE 1 – INVERNESS TO GARVE

(accommodation, refreshments, camping 4 miles off-route in Beauly, cycle shop, station).

Muir of Ord (pop 2500) is the site of the Black Isle show, the largest agricultural show in northern

Scotland, which is held on the showgrounds south of the town during the first weekend of August. The Black Isle, an agricultural area north of Inverness, is a major producer of barley. Much of this is taken to the Glen Ord distillery, one of only a handful of Scottish distilleries to retain its own dedicated maltings. Here it is used to produce both Singleton single malt whisky (an export-only product) and whisky for blending into Johnnie Walker brands. Opened in 1838, Glen Ord, which is nowadays owned by Diageo, is the fourth largest distillery in Scotland producing nearly 11 million litres per year from 14 pot stills. There is a visitor centre that arranges tours of the distillery and adjoining bonded warehouse.

Go ahead over crossroads and pass station L. Turn L (West Rd, A832, sp Marybank) and continue past **Glen Ord distillery** L and through **Urray** (accommodation) to reach **Marybank** (16 miles, 25m) (accommodation). Follow main road bearing R at crossroads and continue on Moy bridge over river Conon to reach T-junction. Turn L (A835, sp Contin) through **Contin** (18.5 miles, 29m) (accommodation, refreshments, camping, cycle shop 3 miles uphill off-route in Strathpeffer).

Cross river Black Water and soon join cycle track L. Pass through Achilty (accommodation) and continue on road through forested gorge of river Black Water, passing **Rogie falls** R. ◄ Continue through **Tarvie** (refreshments) and along shore of Loch Garve R to reach **Garve** (24.5 miles, 72m) (station) where stage ends in front of former hotel.

> Rogie falls are a spectacular sight when the Black Water is in spate. During August and September, salmon leaping up the falls can be seen from a suspension bridge over the river.

STAGE 2
Garve to Lochcarron

Start	Garve hotel (72m)
Finish	Lochcarron hotel (5m)
Distance	36.5 miles (58.5km)
Ascent	214m
Descent	281m
Waymarking	NC500, following A832 to Achnasheen then A890 to Lochcarron

Quiet main roads are followed on this stage, climbing gently up Strath Bran then descending equally gently down Strath Carron following the route of the Inverness to Kyle of Lochalsh railway. Both sparsely populated valleys have a series of small pretty lochs. Most of the road, originally built by Thomas Telford in the early 19th century, was widened and straightened in the 1990s although the last few miles after Achnashellach remain single lane with passing places.

From hotel in **Garve**, follow main road (A835) NW parallel with railway L. After end of village, fork L (A832, sp Gairloch) at **Gorstan** road junction. Continue through forest to spread out hamlet of **Lochluichart** (5 miles,

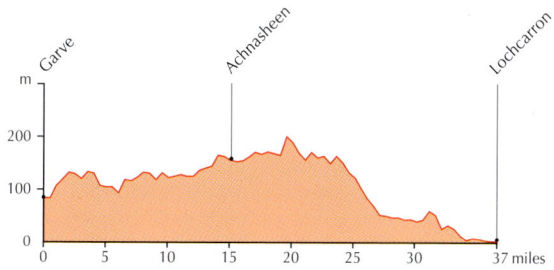

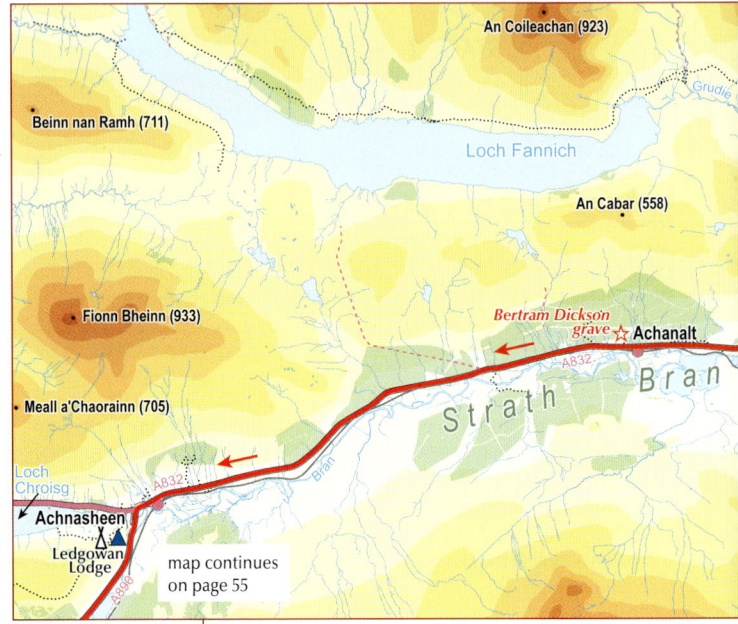

102m) (accommodation, station), with loch below L. Pass Grudie Bridge power station R and continue beside Loch a'Chuilinn L to **Achanalt** (9.5 miles, 125m) (station).

In Achanalt, the Croc na Bhain burial ground on a hillside just right of the main road holds the **grave of Captain Bertram Dickson** (1873–1913), a pioneer aviator and the first British serviceman to gain a pilot's licence (1910). He took part in early flying displays including an exercise on Salisbury plain that was watched by Winston Churchill and Lord Kitchener and led to the formation of the Royal Flying Corps, a precursor of the RAF. While flying in Milan, he was involved in the first recorded mid-air collision and although he survived, serious injuries contributed to his death three years later. Nowadays

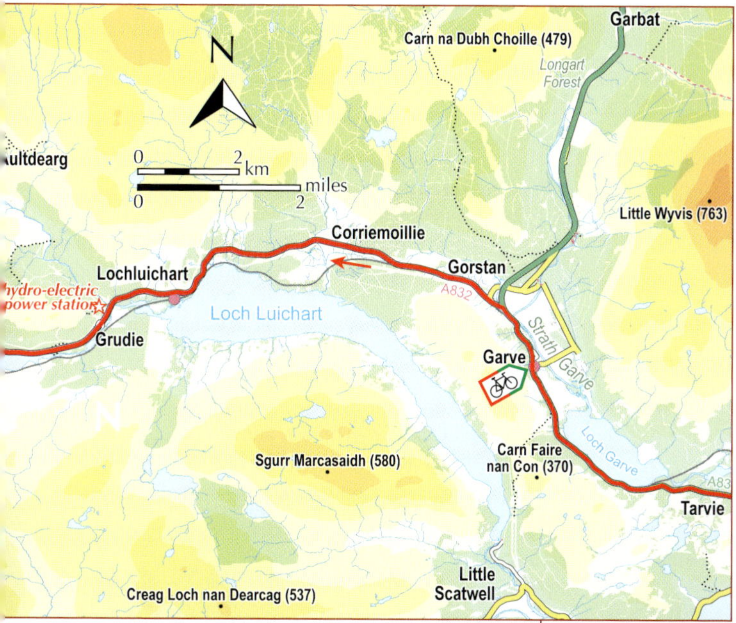

STAGE 2 – GARVE TO LOCHCARRON

Pioneer military aviator Bertram Dickson is buried at Achanalt

the skies above Strath Bran are used by the RAF for low-level fighter pilot training and it is said passing jets dip their wings in salute to Dickson.

Continue through Strath Bran valley, with forested hillsides R and river meandering along valley floor L, to reach **Achnasheen** (16 miles, 155m) (accommodation, hostel, refreshments, camping, station). Fork L at roundabout (A890, first exit, sp Lochcarron) and cross river Bran. Pass Ledgowan Lodge hotel R and follow road ascending gently past Loch Gowan L to reach summit (19.5 miles, 197m) then descend past Loch Sgamhain L into Strath Carron. Cycle through **Craig** (hostel) and under railway bridge to reach spread out community of **Achnashellach** (28.5 miles, 42m) (station). Continue beside Loch Dùghaill L then cross railway and pass through **Balnacra** and **Coulags**. Road continues through forestry plantations

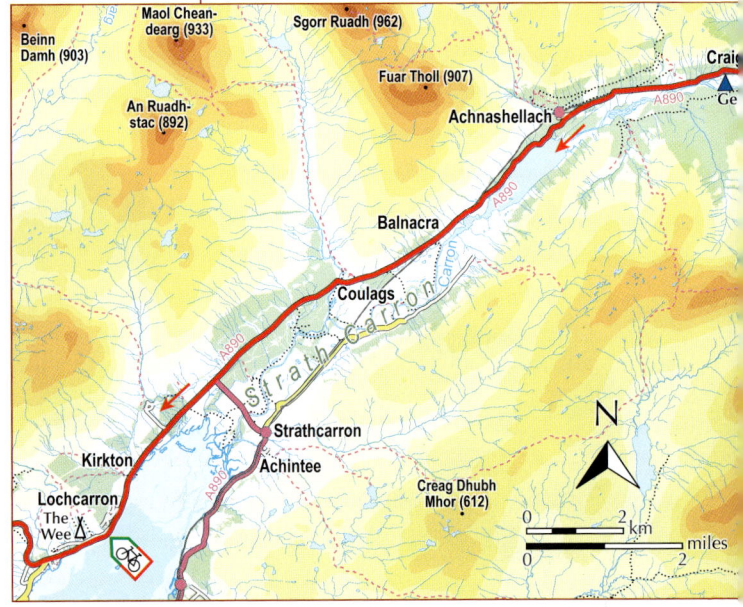

STAGE 2 – GARVE TO LOCHCARRON

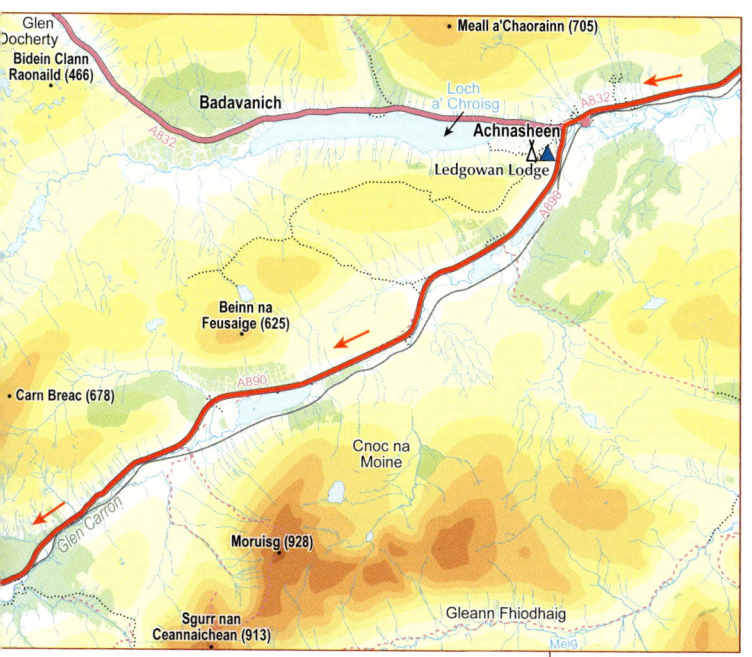

to reach Strathcarron junction (34 miles, 7m). ▶ Keep ahead, passing salt flats and golf course (both L) and church R to reach **Lochcarron village** (36.5 miles, 5m) (accommodation, refreshments, camping) where stage ends on lochside in front of hotel.

Turn R to reach Strathcarron village after 1 mile (accommodation, refreshments, station).

LOCHCARRON VILLAGE

Lochcarron village (pop 925), which spreads for over 2 miles along the north shore of Loch Carron sea loch, developed after the parliamentary road was opened in 1813. In the 19th century, copper and iron ore were mined around Loch Kishorn but yields were low and the last mine closed over 100 years ago. Nowadays the main employment is in tourism and crofting. Although Lochcarron Weavers has an eponymous name, it is merely a retail outlet for the world's leading manufacturer of tartan based in the Scottish Borders and weaving no longer takes place here.

STAGE 3
Lochcarron to Shieldaig (direct route)

Start	Lochcarron hotel (5m)
Finish	Shieldaig, Tigh an Eilean hotel (4m)
Distance	15.5 miles (25km)
Ascent	301m
Descent	302m
Waymarking	None, follow A896

There are two very different choices of route for this stage. This route is recommended for cyclists as it takes a quiet main road over a low pass directly from Loch Kishorn to the small coastal village of Shieldaig. The alternative via Applecross (Stage 3A) climbs very steeply (20 per cent in places) over the Bealach na Bà pass.

Alternative route (Stage 3A) over Bealach na Bà turns L here.

From hotel in **Lochcarron** follow A896 W along Lochside. At end of village, road ascends steeply over Torra Fionn (145m) then descends through Cumhang a' Ghlinne gorge to **Ardarroch** (hostel, refreshments) above the shore of Loch Kishorn. Follow road bearing R beside salt marshes L to reach road junction L beside café in **Tornapress** (7 miles, 3m) (refreshments). ◄

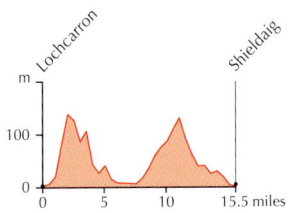

The dry dock at Loch Kishorn is used to maintain off-shore oil rigs

When **North Sea oil exploration** was extended in the 1970s from coastal waters into greater depths, larger drilling platforms were needed. As it had deep water, Loch Kishorn was chosen as the site for a yard building new oil rigs. A dry dock was constructed and 3000 employees were housed in two old liners moored offshore. When the Ninian Central platform was launched in 1978, its 600,000 tonnes made this steel and concrete construction the world's heaviest ever moveable object. In 1992 the yard was used to prefabricate parts for the Skye bridge but when this was completed the yard closed. It reopened in 2019 and in addition to maintaining oil rigs it it used for the construction of both off-shore wind farms and sea pens for fish farming.

Continue ahead on A896 (sp Shieldaig, do not cross bridge) and pass Kinloch Damph fish farm L. Ascend steadily past series of small lochs R to reach summit (11 miles, 135m). Continue ahead, now descending through Glen Shieldaig and pass road junction L. ▶

Follow road alongside Loch Shieldaig L and just before road starts ascending, fork L following shore road

Alternative route over Bealach na Bà rejoins here.

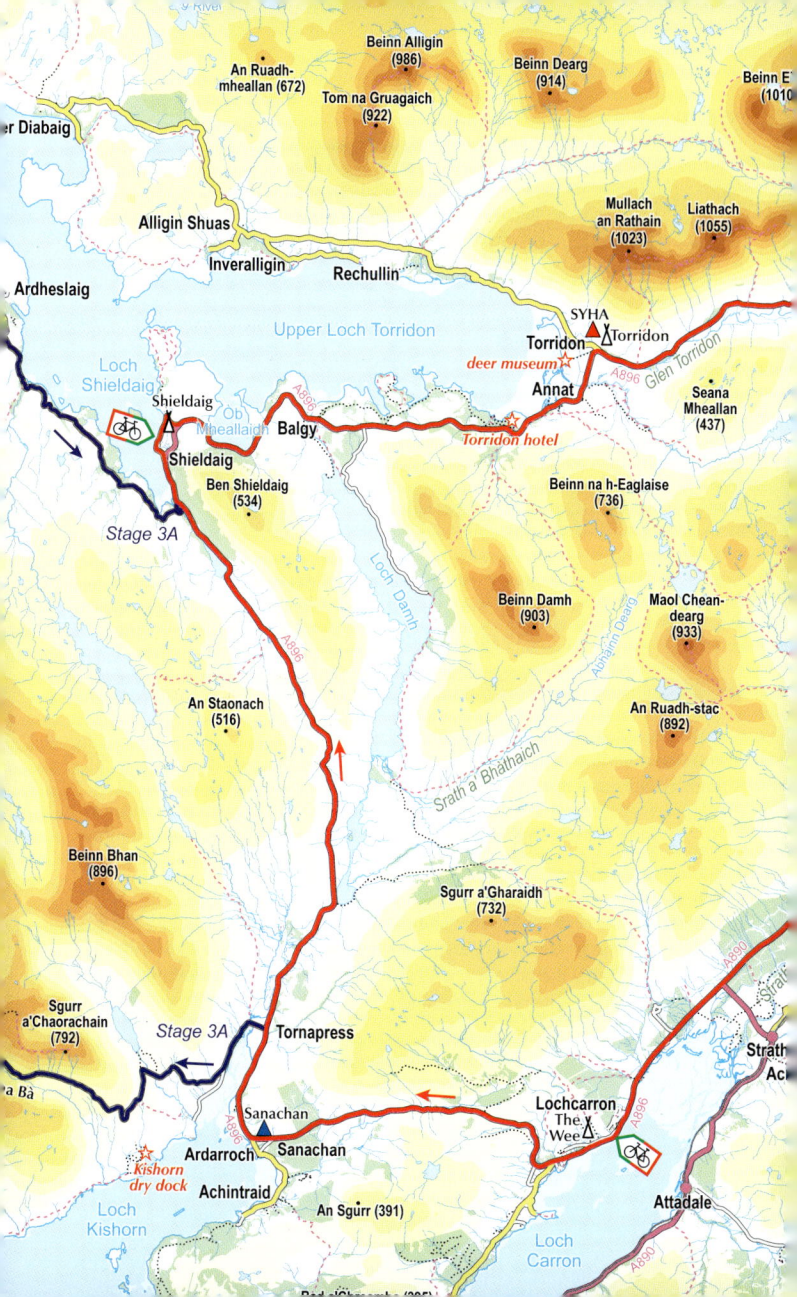

The Scots pines on Shieldaig island were planted for use in shipbuilding

over cattle grid into **Shieldaig village** (15.5 miles, 4m) (accommodation, refreshments, camping) where stage ends outside Tigh an Eilean hotel.

SHIELDAIG

Shieldaig (pop 85) was a planned fishing village constructed (1810) during the Napoleonic Wars with the intention of providing a reserve of seamen who could serve in the Royal Navy during times of conflict. As part of the same scheme, the road from Kishorn (nowadays the A896) was built to allow access and trees were planted on offshore Shieldaig island to provide timber for boats. Fish prices were guaranteed and salt for preserving the catch was provided free. However, the war finished long before the scheme was completed and any seamen had been trained. Nowadays prawns and mussels are landed, but the principal employment is tourism. The Scots pines planted on Shieldaig island were never harvested and the island is now a nature reserve with sea eagles, guillemots, otters and other creatures.

STAGE 3A
Lochcarron to Shieldaig (via Applecross)

Start	Lochcarron hotel (5m)
Finish	Shieldaig, Tigh an Eilean hotel (4m)
Distance	42.5 miles (68.5km)
Ascent	1292m
Descent	1293m
Waymarking	NC500
Note	See Stage 3 for map

This alternative route climbs steeply (20 per cent in places) on a narrow winding road over the Bealach na Bà pass, the steepest and third highest mountain road in Scotland, to reach Applecross. It then follows a frequently undulating coastal road around a sparsely populated peninsula to the small coastal village of Shieldaig.

From Lochcarron hotel follow instructions for Stage 3 to reach road junction L beside café in **Tornapress** (7 miles,

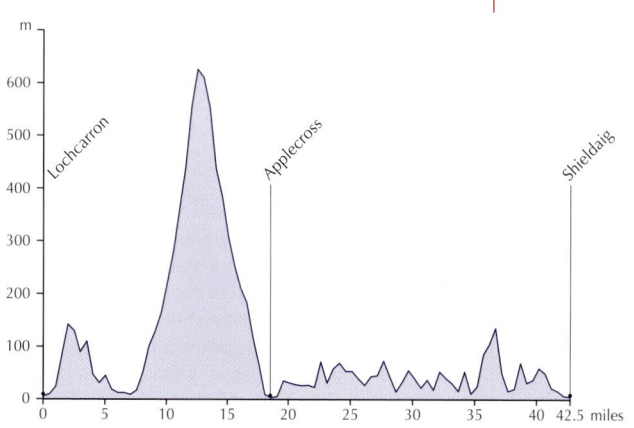

The narrow road over Bealach na Bà pass has a maximum gradient of 20 per cent

3m) (refreshments) where road sign warns of difficult road conditions on Bealach na Bá pass.

The **Bealach na Bà** is a difficult and challenging ride over a very steep mountain pass much used by cars, motorcaravans and motorbikes. The road is so narrow that it is often impossible to overtake between passing places, which are up to 200 metres apart, causing queues of frustrated motorists to build up behind slowly ascending cyclists. Visibility is often poor, made worse by low cloud, with descending vehicles suddenly appearing out of the mist. Lights, reflectors and a high-vis jacket are essential in poor weather.

Turn L (sp Applecross), then cross Tornapress bridge over river Kishorn and soon start ascending. Road climbs steadily at first but becomes much steeper when it reaches Coire na Bà. At head of corrie, pass round three tight hairpins where maximum gradient of 20 per cent is reached for short distance before ascent eases as road reaches the shoulder of Sgurr a' Chaorachain mountain and summit at **Carn Glas** (13 miles, 626m). Descend

STAGE 3A – LOCHCARRON TO SHIELDAIG (VIA APPLECROSS)

steeply to **Applecross** (18 miles, 5m) (accommodation, hostel, refreshments, camping) on shore of Inner Sound.

APPLECROSS

Applecross (pop 550) is a small village with a view across Inner Sound to Raasay island with the Cuillin mountains of Skye rising behind. Until the mid-1970s, the only approach was by sea or via road over the Bealach na Bà (Pass of the cattle in English). Originally a drove road, the Bealach was converted into a parliamentary road in 1822, although it remained dirt surfaced until it was asphalted in the 1950s. As the road is often impassable in winter, the village could become cut off for many weeks. The Applecross coastal road was opened in 1976, originally to serve a military underwater testing establishment at Sand. In May and September two cycling events (the Bealach Beag and Bealach Mór) that include ascents of the Bealach in their itineraries are held.

Applecross house, built in 1740 for the MacKenzie family, has an attractive walled garden

Turn R and follow coastal road around bay, passing **Applecross house** R. Continue N, close to but above Inner Sound, passing turn-off L for **BUTEC testing station** at Sand. ▶ Road moves away from coast and continues past **Lonbain**, **Callakille** L (26 miles, 28m) and **Cuaig**. Route now heads inland cutting off northern tip of Applecross peninsula and crossing low summit before descending past **Fearnmore** L (30.5 miles, 45m), which faces E across Loch Torridon. Continue past **Fearnbeg** L and **Arrina** L then climb over low headland and descend

BUTEC (British Underwater Test and Evaluation Centre) tests torpedoes and sonar tracking systems for the MOD. The range occupies a 6-mile by 4-mile sea area just off the coast.

Shieldaig village seen across Loch Shieldaig

Direct route from Lochcarron is rejoined here.

past **Kenmore** L (34.5 miles, 24m). Landscape becomes more rugged as road climbs over another headland (summit 139m) then descends steeply past **Ardheslaig** (37.5 miles, 19m). Undulate over three more low headlands before descending round hairpins to T-junction in Glen Shieldaig and turn L (A896, sp Shieldaig). ◄

Follow road alongside Loch Shieldaig L and just before road starts ascending, fork L following shore road over cattle grid into **Shieldaig village** (42.5 miles, 4m) (accommodation, refreshments, camping) where stage ends outside Tigh an Eilean hotel.

STAGE 4
Shieldaig to Gairloch

Start	Shieldaig, Tigh an Eilean hotel (4m)
Finish	Gairloch, The Gale heritage centre (12m)
Distance	36.5 miles (58.5km)
Ascent	597m
Descent	589m
Waymarking	NC500, following A896 to Kinlochewe then A832 to Gairloch

This stage circles the Torridon range, following quiet main roads along three thinly populated glens while climbing gently over and descending from two low summits. Throughout the stage there are spectacular views of the Torridon mountains and later of Loch Maree, the largest Scottish loch north of Inverness.

From Tigh an Eilean hotel in **Shieldaig** follow lochside road N then turn sharply R in front of primary school and follow road uphill to T-junction. Turn L (A896, sp Torridon) and follow road contouring along hillside overlooking Upper Loch Torridon below with views of

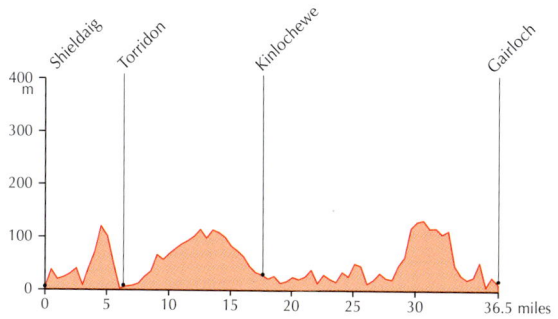

CYCLING THE NORTH COAST 500

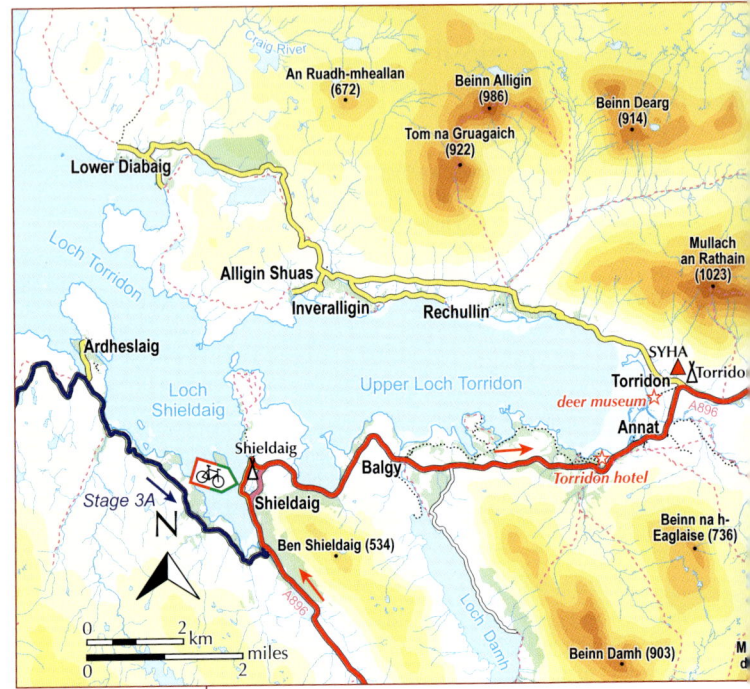

Torridon village, which sits below the towers and buttresses of Liathach (1055m), is a popular climbing and walking centre complete with a National Trust information centre and a deer park with a deer museum.

Beinn Alligin (986m) opposite. Pass **Balgy** L, then climb over headland (119m) and descend past Torridon hotel (accommodation, refreshments) L into **Annat** (6 miles, 5m). Continue over river Torridon to reach road junction L for **Torridon village** (7.5 miles, 12m) (accommodation, hostel, refreshments, camping). ◄

Bear R (still A896, sp Kinlochewe) and follow road ascending gently along **Glen Torridon** with river Torridon R and first Liathach (1055m) then Beinn Eighe (1010m) rising L. At head of valley (13 miles, 111m), pass **Loch Clair** R and descend A' Ghairbhe valley to reach T-junction in **Kinlochewe** (17 miles, 32m) (accommodation, hostel, refreshments, camping).

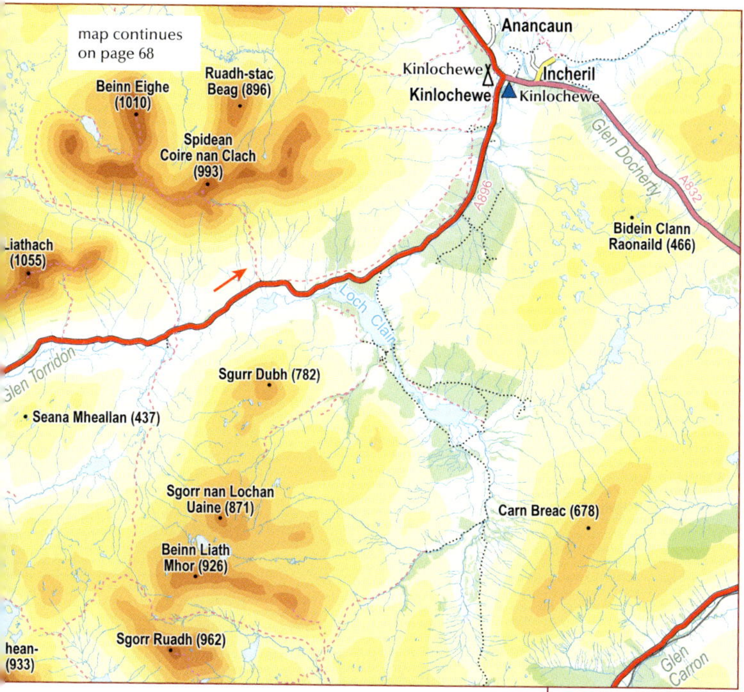

STAGE 4 – SHIELDAIG TO GAIRLOCH

Cycling towards Liathach (photo credit: Richard Barrett)

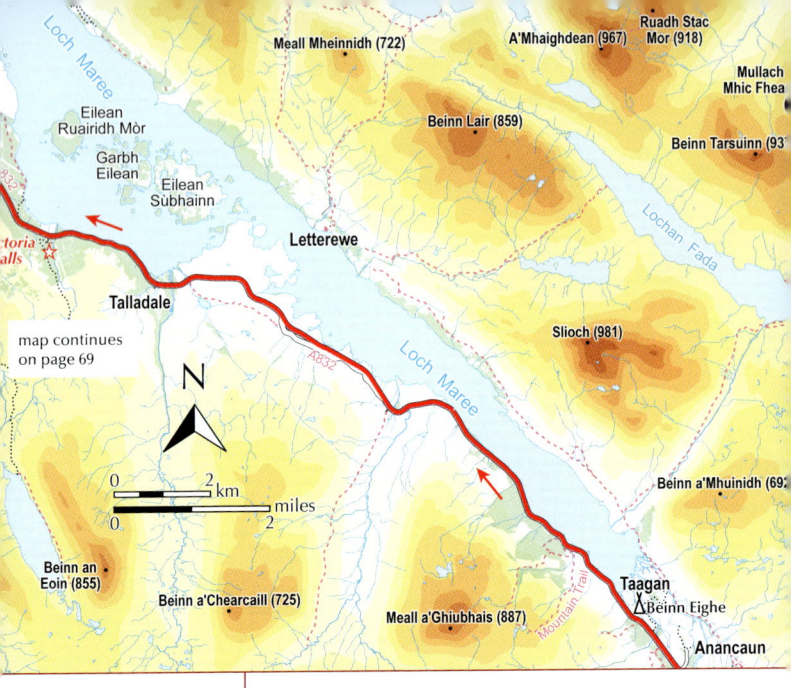

Turn L (A832, sp Gairloch) and pass **Taagan** R (18.5 miles, 23m) (camping). Continue beside Loch Maree to reach **Talladale** (26.5 miles, 14m) (accommodation, refreshments).

LOCH MAREE

Loch Maree, the largest loch north of Loch Ness, is often referred to as the most beautiful loch in the Scottish Highlands. Overlooked by Beinn Eighe (1010m, west) and Slioch (981m, east), the loch holds five wooded islands and many smaller ones. The largest island, Eilean Sùbhainn, is the only island in Britain that contains a loch that itself holds another island. Smaller Isle Maree has a ruined chapel, graveyard and well, said to be the hermitage of the Irish saint Màel Ruba (AD642–722), founder of Applecross monastery. The loch is an important fishery, with salmon and sea trout returning from the sea every summer to spawn. The British record weight sea trout (8.8kg) was caught here in 1952, but it is not just humans who fish here as the

STAGE 4 – SHIELDAIG TO GAIRLOCH

salmon are also food for otters and black-throated divers that nest on the islands. The lake has a population of Arctic Char while golden eagles inhabit the surrounding heights. The lake became popular after 1877 when Queen Victoria visited and stayed in the hotel, while further fame came in 1966 when a record 'Loch Maree Islands', by the accordionist Fergie MacDonald, topped the Scottish pop charts.

Continue through Slattadale forest, passing **Victoria falls** L. ▶ Ascend steadily out of forest to summit (131m), then descend past Loch Bad an Sgalaig and continue downhill following river Kerry L through Glen Kerry. Pass **Kerrysdale** R and continue to **Charlestown** (35.5 miles, 5m) (accommodation, refreshments) on the shore of Loch Gairloch. Follow main road over low headland and along lochside to Auchtercairn in centre of **Gairloch** (36.5 miles, 12m) (accommodation, hostel, refreshments, camping, tourist office) where stage ends outside 'The Gale' heritage centre.

> Victoria falls were named in honour of Queen Victoria's visit to Loch Maree.

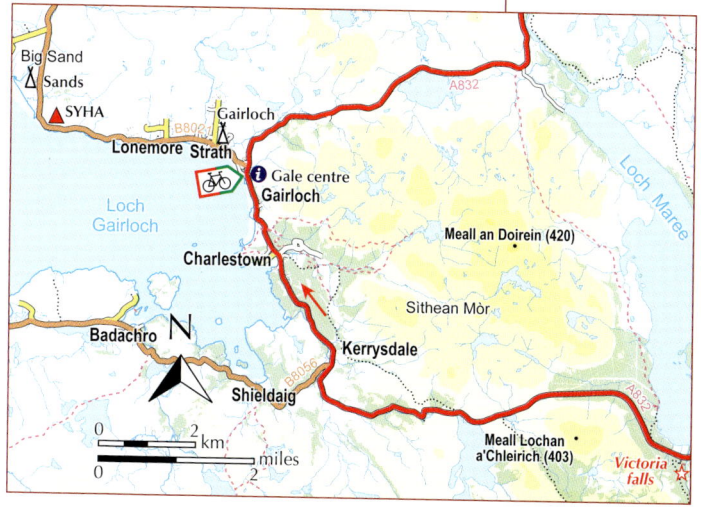

GAIRLOCH

Gairloch village consists of three adjoining communities stretched alongside the loch

Gairloch (pop 600) consists of three small communities (Charlestown, Auchtercairn and Strath) spread around the head of the eponymous loch. A mild micro-climate, abundant fishing and a sheltered bay have attracted settlement starting in Neolithic times and including Bronze Age, Iron Age, Picts and Vikings to present-day Scots. Road access is a fairly new addition and earlier residents probably arrived by sea. Since the 15th century, the land around Gairloch has been owned by Clan Mackenzie. During the 19th-century clearances, Sir Hector Mackenzie refused to evict any tenants, maintaining a thriving community that still continues today. Changes have happened, however, in employment patterns where fishing has declined while tourism and hospitality have become the main sources of income. A few boats still catch shellfish but others operate as tourist boats on wildlife trips to see whales, dolphins, seals and seabirds.

STAGE 5
Gairloch to Ullapool

Start	Gairloch, The Gale heritage centre (12m)
Finish	Ullapool, Shore St junction (9m)
Distance	55 miles (88.5km)
Ascent	1078m
Descent	1081m
Waymarking	NC500, following A832 to Braemore then A835 to Ullapool

This frequently undulating stage opens on quiet main roads that first circle the northern part of the Fisherfield peninsula then follows the river Dundonnell up Strath Beag and crosses a low pass before descending into Strath More. A busier road is then followed beside Loch Broom to reach Ullapool. There is spectacular scenery of lochs and mountains throughout and two popular gardens at Poolewe and Leckmelm where non-native plants are able to flourish due to the moderating effect of the Gulf Stream.

From outside 'The Gale' heritage centre in **Gairloch**, follow A832 N bearing R away from Lochside and ascending steeply with views back over Gairloch. Gradient

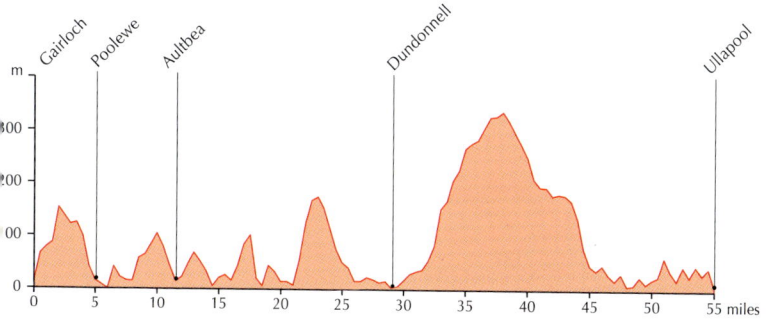

Cycling the North Coast 500

eases as road continues up valley of Abhainn Achadh a' Chairn to reach summit (141m) with view ahead of Fisherfield range and An Teallach behind. Continue past

STAGE 5 – GAIRLOCH TO ULLAPOOL

Loch Tollaidh R then descend into River Ewe valley, passing Tollie where there is view R over N end of Loch Maree. Follow river R and fork R over bridge through

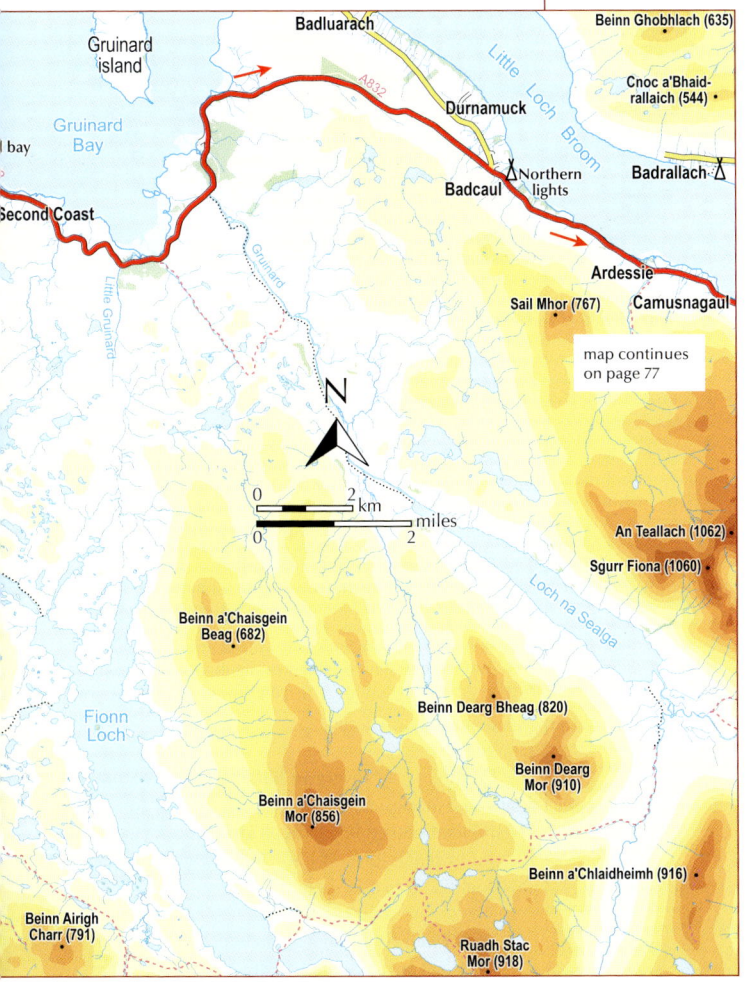

Exotic plants at Inverewe gardens survive the winter because of mild weather brought by the Gulf Stream

Poolewe (5.5 miles, 9m) (accommodation, refreshments, camping).

Inverewe botanic gardens, which were created by Osgood Mackenzie between 1862–1922 on a formerly barren hillside, are planted with over 2500 exotic plants on the 20ha (49-acre) site. An additional 800ha (2000 acres) of woodland is managed for conservation and recreation. A mild micro-climate (due to the influence of the Gulf Stream) and a sheltered location allow plants from all over the world to grow and flourish providing a riot of colour especially in spring and early summer. The estate was gifted to the National Trust by Mackenzie's daughter in 1952 and has become a popular tourist destination.

Continue past **Inverewe botanic gardens** L and follow road alongside Loch Ewe, ascending to summit (103m) then descending through **Drumchork** (accommodation) to reach turn-off L for **Aultbea** (12 miles, 24m) (accommodation, refreshments).

Loch Ewe was an important anchorage for Royal Navy and merchant ships during World War II when

Stage 5 – Gairloch to Ullapool

harbours on Scotland's east coast were judged vulnerable to attack by German bombers based in Norway. To counter this, alternate anchorages were developed on the west coast, one of these being in Loch Ewe offshore from Aultbea. The loch entrance was protected by submarine netting, while anti-aircraft batteries were built along the shore. After Russia entered the war, the loch became a rendezvous point and facilities base for naval ships escorting Arctic convoys to Murmansk. Of the 489 merchant vessels in 19 convoys that left here between February 1942 and December 1944, only 16 were sunk. The small Russian Arctic Convoy museum beside the main road describes the wartime activities in Loch Ewe. Post war, the loch is still used by the navy with a refuelling base at Drumchork for use by NATO ships during naval exercises.

Continue ahead, climbing over low headland and descending to small village of **Laide** (14 miles, 29m) (accommodation, refreshments, camping) overlooking Gruinard bay. ▶ Bear R and follow undulating road through First Coast, then ascend through **Second Coast**

Ruined Laide church is claimed to be Scotland's oldest, built in the sixth century by Saint Columba. However, it was greatly restored in the 18th century then abandoned in the 19th century.

Ruined Laide church is claimed to have been built for Saint Columba in the sixth century

THE ISLAND OF GRUINARD

Gruinard island was used to test biological weapons during World War II

The small island of Gruinard lies about half a mile offshore in Gruinard bay. In 1942, during World War II, it was requisitioned by the Ministry of Defence in order to determine the effect of an attack using biological weapons containing anthrax. A flock of sheep was taken to the island where a small bomb containing anthrax spores was detonated. Within days the sheep became infected and eventually all died. Attempts to decontaminate the island after the experiment proved unsuccessful and scientists concluded that anywhere subject to an anthrax bomb would remain uninhabitable for decades. Gruinard was closed to visitors and remained so until 1986, when another clean-up exercise was undertaken. The island was sprayed with formaldehyde and contaminated top-soil removed. In 1990 it was declared free of contamination and sold back to the original owners for the 1942 purchase price of £500. Sheep were reintroduced to graze the island, and there have been no cases of anthrax.

to summit (112m). Descend steeply (12%) to cross Little Gruinard river. Undulate over another headland then descend to cross river Gruinard and pass Gruinard house L.

STAGE 5 – GAIRLOCH TO ULLAPOOL

Bear R away from loch and follow long steady ascent over open moorland to summit (176m) with view ahead over Little Loch Broom. Descend through **Badcaul** (24.5 miles, 78m) (camping). Continue along loch shore

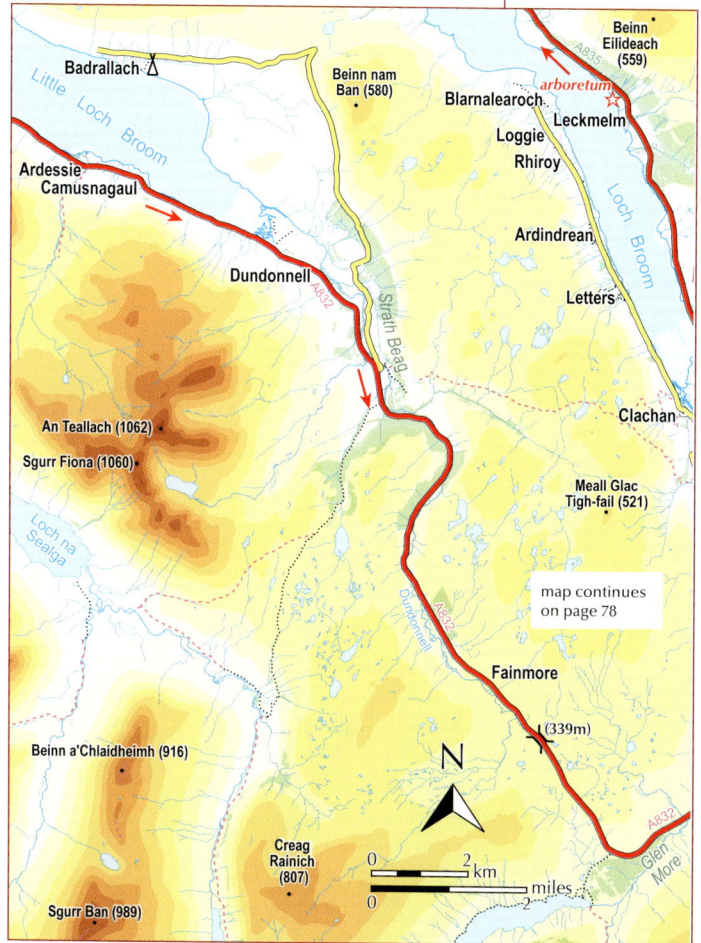

Cycling the North Coast 500

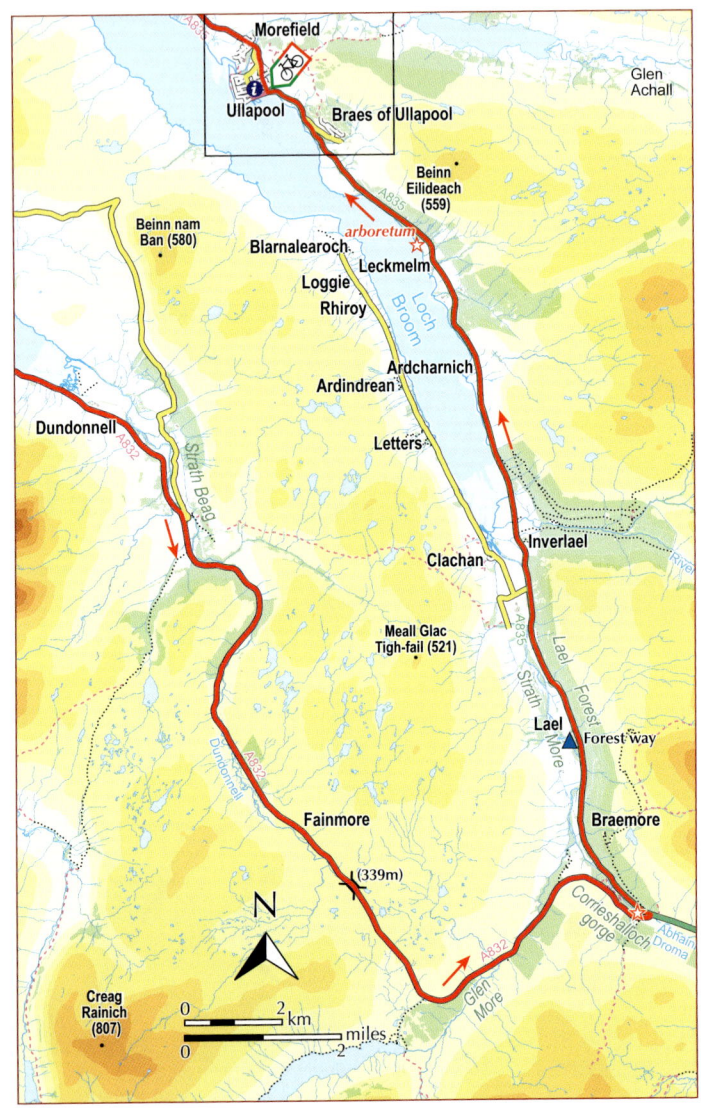

STAGE 5 – GAIRLOCH TO ULLAPOOL

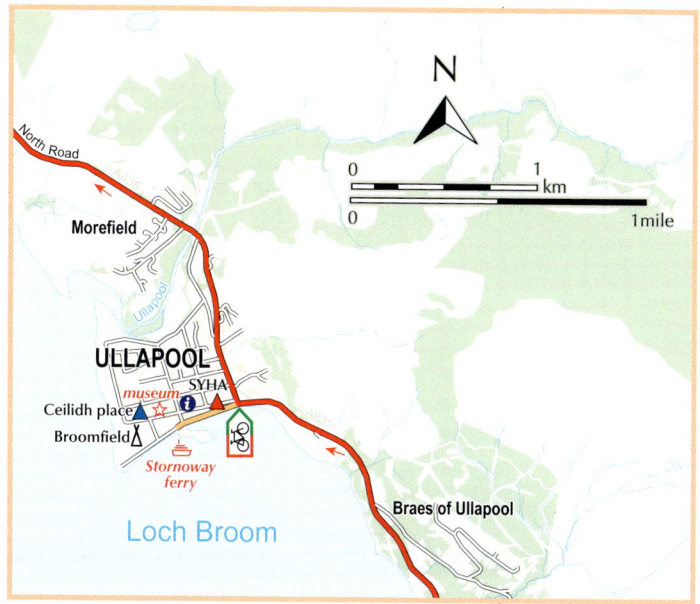

through Badbea, **Ardessie** and **Camusnagaul** (27.5 miles, 16m) (accommodation) to reach **Dundonnell** (29.5 miles, 4m) (accommodation, refreshments) at head of loch with An Teallach (1062m) rising R.

Follow road ascending steadily through forested Strath Beag beside river Dundonnell, then cross river at Fain bridge and continue across open moorland past ruined building at Fainmore to reach summit (38 miles, 339m). Cycle downhill, descending through forest into Glen More to reach visitor centre for **Corrieshalloch gorge nature reserve** L at Braemore junction (43 miles, 184m). ▶

Turn L (A835), passing above other side of gorge and descend steeply (12%) through Strath More passing **Braemore** and **Lael** (accommodation, hostel) to reach head of Loch Broom. Continue undulating through tiny

A path from the visitor centre winds down into Corrieshalloch gorge to reach a footbridge over the 46m-high Falls of Measach and a viewpoint below.

lochside communities of **Ardcharnich** (50.5 miles, 28m) and **Leckmelm** (51.5 miles, 36m).

> The **arboretum at Leckmelm** is contemporary with Poolewe, being laid out between 1879 and 1930 on a southwest-facing slope overlooking Loch Broom. It contains a collection of trees and shrubs collected from temperate zones all around the world including monkey puzzle, cedars, cypress, wellingtonia and 12 species of rhododendron. Two of the trees are 'champions', the tallest known examples of their species in the world. A network of paths winds through the gardens, which are open to visitors.

Pass arboretum L and continue beside loch past housing development at **Braes of Ullapool** (accommodation) on hillside R to reach road junction with Shore St at beginning of **Ullapool** (55 miles, 9m) (accommodation, hostel, refreshments, camping, tourist office).

ULLAPOOL

Ullapool (pop 1500), the major town of the northwest coast, sits on the north side of Loch Broom. Although a small settlement existed prior to the 18th century (including the oldest building, a ruined catholic chapel) most of the town was built in 1788 as a herring port for the British Fisheries Society. The grid layout of the town, harbour, church, salt warehouse/customs house and road connecting Ullapool with the south were all designed by Thomas Telford. Nowadays it is still a small fishing port but it is also a tourist centre and ferry terminal for boats to Stornoway on the Isle of Lewis. The Gulf Stream moderates winter temperatures enabling exotic plants such as New Zealand cabbage trees (often wrongly called palms) to survive.

STAGE 6
Ullapool to Lochinver

Start	Ullapool, Shore St junction (9m)
Finish	Lochinver, war memorial (4m)
Distance	35.5 miles (57km) or 30 miles (48.5km) via Loch Lurgainn
Ascent	606m or 764m via Loch Lurgainn
Descent	611m or 769m via Loch Lurgainn
Waymarking	NC500, following A835 to Ledmore then A837 to Lochinver

This stage climbs away from the coast following a quiet main road onto a plateau of wild open land covered with lochs and lochans. The Moine thrust fault line is crossed as the route passes Ben More Assynt before following Loch Assynt and the river Inver back to the sea at Lochinver. There are a few ascents and descents near the beginning but thereafter most of the stage is level or gently rolling. An alternative route avoids the main road by following an undulating country road alongside Loch Lurgainn and across the southern part of the Assynt peninsula.

From Shore St road junction in **Ullapool**, follow Mill St (A835, sp Lochinver) N past high school R. Cross river Ullapool and pass through **Morefield** (accommodation). Ascend over headland (summit 88m) then undulate over

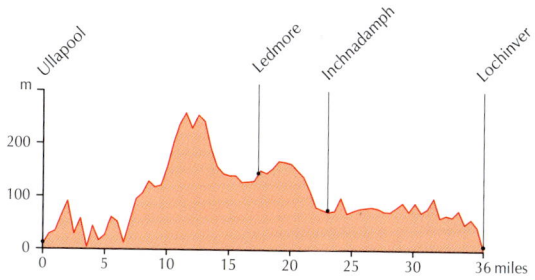

CYCLING THE NORTH COAST 500

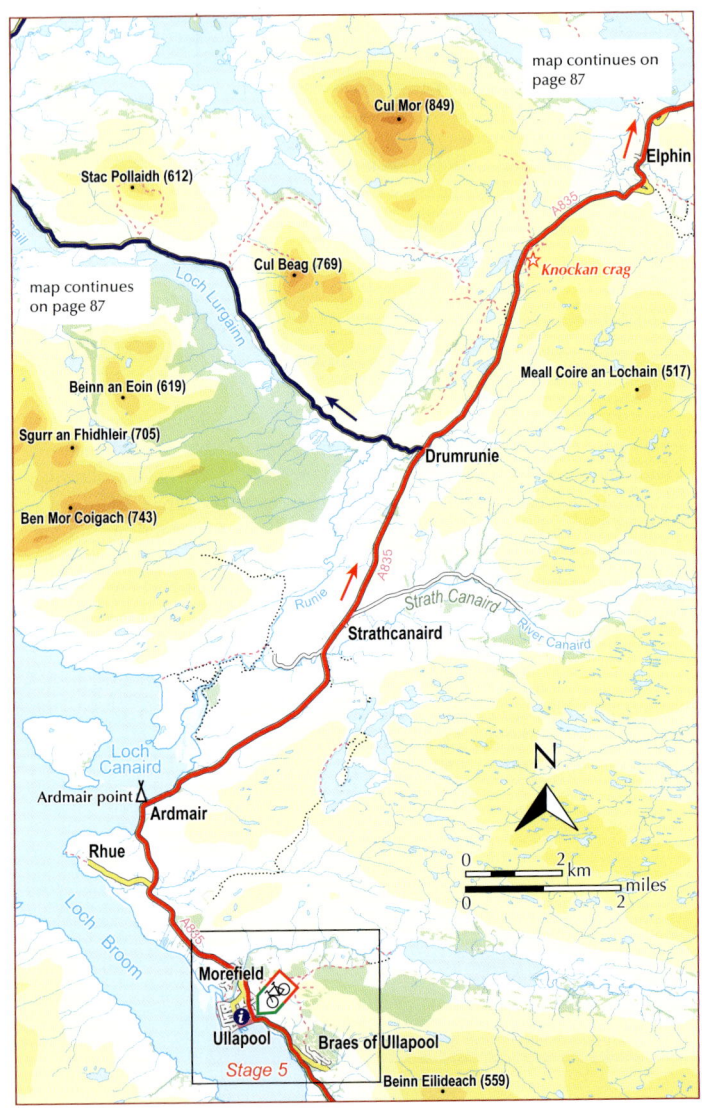

Stage 6 – Ullapool to Lochinver

second (lower) headland before descending to hamlet of **Ardmair** (3.5 miles, 5m) (accommodation, camping) near the mouth of Loch Broom. Road climbs steeply away from coast then continues climbing through narrow gorge before descending to cross river. Ascend steeply past hamlet of **Strathcanaird** (7 miles, 80m) (accommodation) then continue across open moorland to road junction at **Drumrunie** (9.5 miles, 123m).

Alternative route via Loch Lurgainn
Turn L (sp Achiltibuie) and follow narrow country road across open moorland. Descend to run along N shore

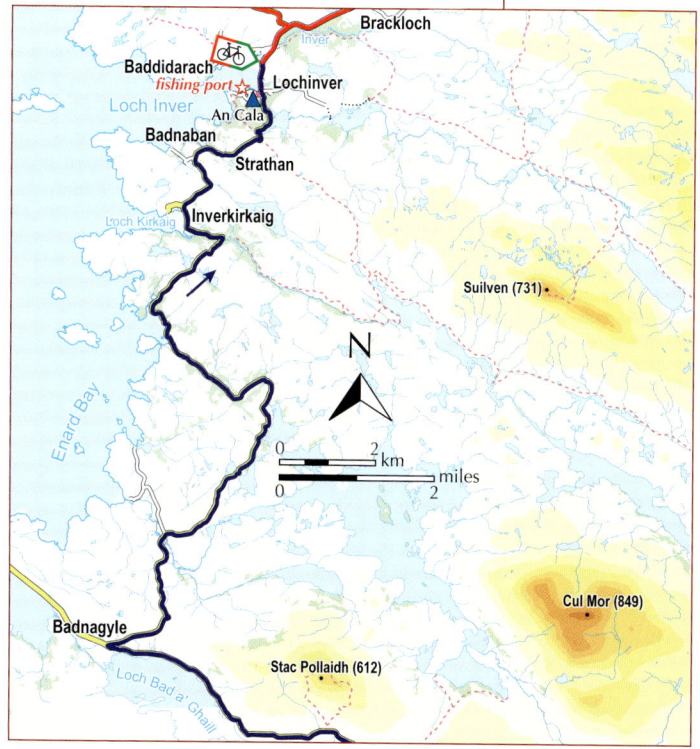

CYCLING THE NORTH COAST 500

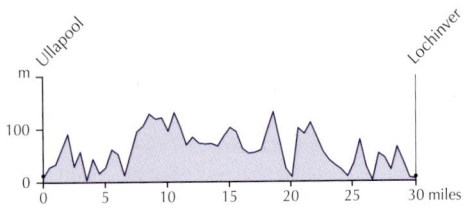

Although not a Munro, Stac Pollaidh is a popular hill with walkers and climbers attracted by an airy walk along its eroded sandstone summit ridge.

of **Loch Lurgainn** with Stac Pollaidh (612m) rising R. ◄ Continue beside Loch Bad a' Ghaill to reach road junction at **Badnagyle** (17.5 miles, 62m) at head of loch. Turn sharply R (sp Inverkirkaig) and ascend over ridge (summit 132m) then descend to fish hatchery in Strath Polly (20 miles, 9m). Landscape becomes more wooded as road climbs steeply over another ridge (summit 103m) then descends into narrow valley and continues to reach sea. Ascend over low ridge and descend to **Inverkirkaig** (27 miles, 3m). Road now undulates gently past small communities of **Badnaban** and **Strathan**, then turns L at traffic lights, passing Lochinver fishing port L to reach **Lochinver** (30 miles, 4m) (accommodation, hostel, refreshments).

Main route via Inchnadamph
Continue ahead (A835), ascending steadily across open moorland dotted with lochans, to reach summit (252m) then pass Knockan crag R and descend steeply to **Elphin** (14.5 miles, 145m) (accommodation, refreshments).

> **Knockan crag** cliffs are part of a geological feature known as the Moine thrust, a fault line that runs across the northwestern tip of Scotland. In the early days of geological study, scientists could not understand why in the region of the fault older quartzite rocks appeared on top of younger sandstone and limestone. The theory of plate tectonics provided a solution to this conundrum. It is believed that over 400 million years ago during the Silurian period, the sideways thrust of the European plate pushed

John Horne and Ben Peach, who developed the theory of plate tectonics, are commemorated at Knockan crag

older rocks 40 miles northwest across Scotland covering younger rocks as it went. There are well-made walks along the crag and an interpretation centre. Local artists have created artworks along the way, the most notable being a huge round boulder sculptured by Joe Smith and known as 'The Globe'.

Continue across moorland to **Ledmore** junction (17.5 miles, 148m). ▶ Turn L at T-junction (A837, sp Lochinver) and follow main road descending through **Stronechrubie**, with Ben More Assynt rising R. Gradient levels off as road continues to **Inchnadamph** (23.5 miles, 73m) (accommodation, hostel, refreshments).

Turn R to reach Altnacealgach (accommodation, refreshments) after 1.5 miles.

Ben More Assynt (996m), another part of the Moine thrust, is topped with a quartzite cap over younger limestone rocks. Water running off from the hard cap has carved an extensive cave network within the limestone. Caves include the 'long cave', which at 5 miles in length is the longest cave in Scotland. In another set of caves near Stonechrubie (known as the 'bone caves'), bones of lynx, brown bear (dated

Cycling the North Coast 500

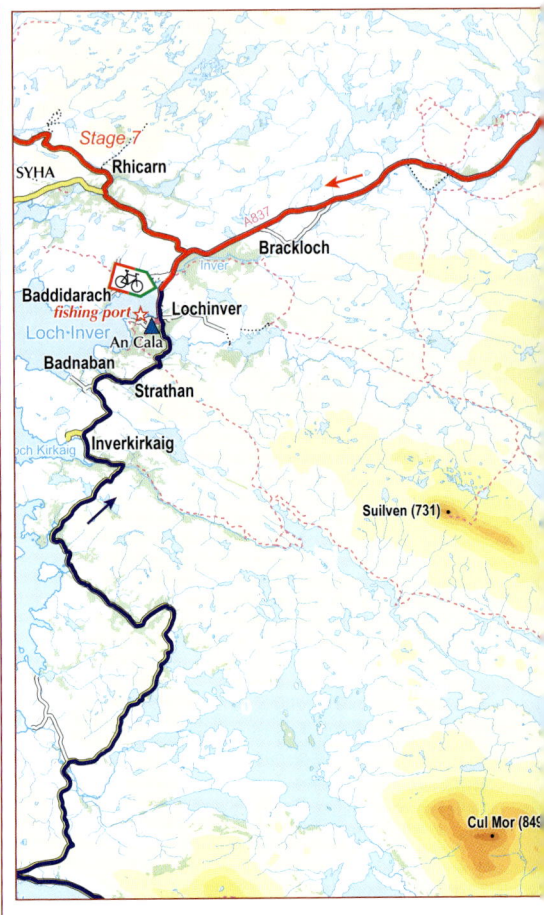

to 11,000 years), arctic fox, reindeer (50,000 years) and polar bear, together with 5000-year-old human skeletons have been found. A monument to the two geologists (John Horne and Ben Peach), who solved the Moine thrust conundrum, stands on a hilltop overlooking Inchnadamph church.

STAGE 6 – ULLAPOOL TO LOCHINVER

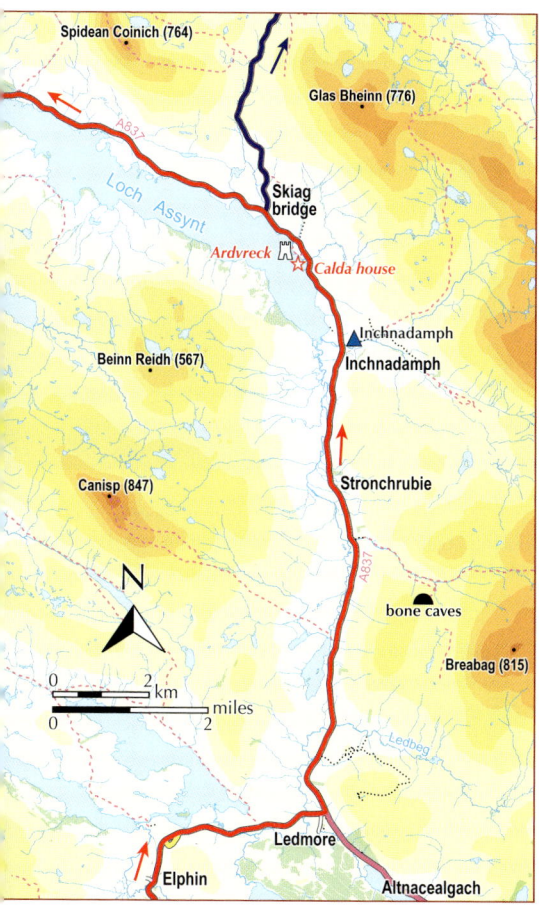

Continue ahead on A837, now along shore of **Loch Assynt** L, passing ruins of **Calda house** beside road L and **Ardvreck castle** on rocky peninsula sticking out into loch. ▶ Bear L at road junction (still A837, sp Lochinver) and cross **Skiag bridge** (25.5 miles, 72m). Follow road along loch shore, passing Little Assynt. Continue across

Built in 1590 by the MacLeods, Ardvreck was captured by the Mackenzies in 1672 then plundered to build nearby Calda house in 1726. Calda itself burnt down in 1737.

Ruined Ardvreck castle sits on the shore of Loch Assynt

To bypass Lochinver and continue onto Stage 7, turn R at road junction (B869, sp Achmelvich).

open country following river Inver to road junction overlooking Lochinver. ◄ Cycle downhill then fork L over river Inver into **Lochinver** (35.5 miles, 4m) (accommodation, hostel, refreshments).

Lochinver (pop 650), which sits below the very recognisable peak of Suilven (731m), is the second largest fishing port in mainland Scotland by weight of catch. The harbour was extended in the 1990s, mainly to cater for French and Spanish fishing boats that land their catch here for onward transportation by road to continental Europe. Land has been cleared for possible future expansion.

STAGE 7
Lochinver to Kylesku

Start	Lochinver, war memorial (4m)
Finish	Kylesku bridge (25m)
Distance	24.5 miles (39.5km) or 19 miles (30.5km) via Skiat bridge
Ascent	770m
Descent	749m
Waymarking	NC500

On this stage a narrow winding minor road is followed circling the Assynt peninsula through a landscape of lochs, cnocs (hillocks) and rocky open moorland passing a few scattered hamlets. This is a challenging stage with the gradient undulating frequently as the road climbs steeply over a series of 100m-plus ridges and descends to sea level between them. If you want to avoid the steep undulations and replace them with one steady climb, an alternative route is available by returning along the A837 to Skiag bridge and then turning left.

ASSYNT

Assynt is a remote peninsula dominated by the three mountains of Suilven, Canisp and Quinag. During the Highland clearances, crofters were relocated to 13 coastal villages, with the cleared land being used for raising livestock. In 1989, a large part of Assynt was sold by its owners, the Vestey family, to a Swedish property company. When the purchasers went bankrupt the estate was put back on the market and eventually bought by an association of local crofters. Its 18,000ha are now managed by the Assynt foundation on behalf of the local community. Most of the landscape is rocky moorland although a few small pockets of ancient Caledonian forest can be found in sheltered glens.

Achmelvich beach, one of many sandy bays in Assynt

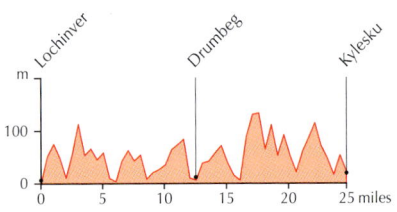

For alternative route, return along A837 to Skiag bridge for 10.5 miles, turn L (A894) through Lairig Unapool pass (260m), between Quinag L and Glas Bheinn R, to reach Kylesku.

Turn L to reach Achmelvich beach (hostel, camping, refreshments) after 2 miles.

◀ From **Lochinver**, follow A837 N out of village, retracing your route if you followed the main route on the previous stage. Pass first turn L then ascend to second turn. Turn L (B869, sp Achmelvich) to follow road across rocky scrubland then descend to pass turn-off for Achmelvich L (2 miles, 7m). ◀ Continue ahead (sp Clachtoll), climbing to summit (113m) then descend to **Clachtoll** (5.5 miles, 13m) (camping) and **Stoer** (6.5 miles, 46m) (hostel).

Climb over low ridge, descending through **Clashnessie** (8.5 miles, 15m) to reach N side of Assynt peninsula. Follow road turning away from coast and undulating over another low headland through **Drumbeg** (13.5 miles, 45m) (accommodation, refreshments). Climb over another ridge then descend steeply through **Nedd** (15 miles, 45m). Road now undulates steeply, climbing and descending over four outlying spurs of Quinag (809m, which rises R), with total ascent (and descent) of 350m, to reach T-junction. Turn L (A894, sp Kylesku)

STAGE 7 – LOCHINVER TO KYLESKU

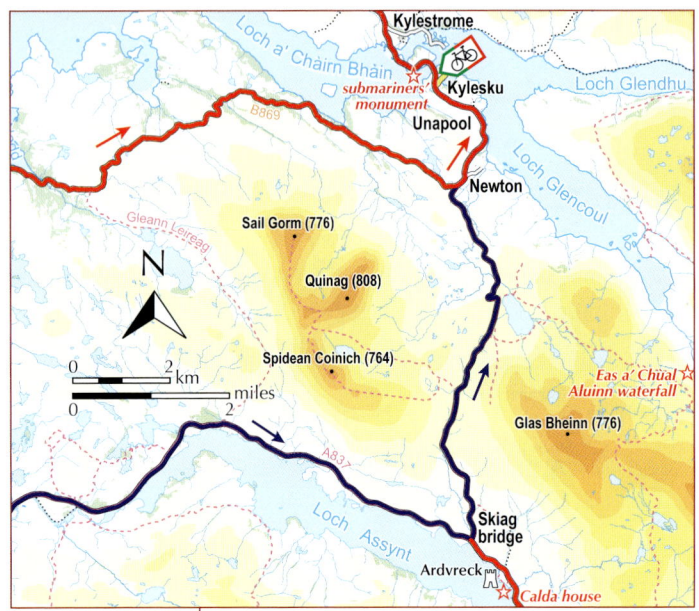

To visit Kylesku village (accommodation, refreshments), turn R 300 metres before the bridge.

downhill past **Newton** R (accommodation, refreshments) and through **Unapool** (23.5 miles, 40m) (accommodation) to reach **Kylesku bridge** (24.5 miles, 25m). ◀

Kylesku bridge opened in 1984, replacing a small vehicular ferry that plied between Kylesku slipway and Kylestrome across a 300-metre channel connecting Loch a' Chàirn Bhàin with Loch Glencoul. The old abandoned ferry can be seen beached opposite the harbour. Kylesku slipway is nowadays used by excursion boats that sail on wildlife watching trips along the rugged coastline to Handa island and Point of Stoer. Sailing the other direction up Loch Glencoul, another boat takes visitors to Eas a' Chùal Aluinn waterfall. With a single vertical drop of 200m, this is the highest waterfall in Britain.

STAGE 8
Kylesku to Durness

Start	Kylesku bridge (25m)
Finish	Durness (40m)
Distance	35 miles (56.5km)
Ascent	714m
Descent	699m
Waymarking	NC500, following A894 to Laxford bridge then A838

This attractive stage follows a quiet main road that undulates through a rocky moorland landscape across the extreme northwest corner of Scotland. Human habitation is limited to two small villages and a few scattered farms.

Cross **Kylesku bridge** and follow A894 N, passing turn-off R for old Kylestrome ferry. ▶ Follow road undulating over rocky moorland past many small lochans then descend to reach former fishing village of **Lower Badcall** (7.5 miles, 25m) (accommodation, refreshments). Climb over more rocky moorland, then descend into **Scourie** (10 miles,

A monument in the car park after the bridge commemorates submariners who trained in the loch to use midget submarines for a 1943 attack in a Norwegian fjord on the German battleship Tirpitz.

Kylesku bridge opened in 1984 to replace a small car ferry

Cycling the North Coast 500

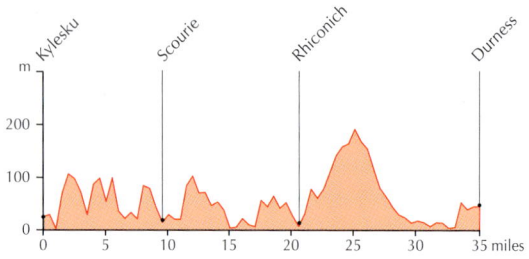

18m) (accommodation, refreshments, camping, cycle shop), overlooking Scourie bay.

Follow road climbing steeply over more rocky moorland then descend past Badnabay to road junction before **Laxford bridge** (16.5 miles, 11m). Keep ahead (A838, sp Durness), crossing river Laxford and continue with quartzite capped Arkle (787m), Foinavon (911m) and Cranstackie (802m) dominating landscape R to reach **Rhiconich** (21 miles, 15m) (accommodation) at head of Loch Inchard.

Continue across wild moorland, ascending steadily to summit at **Gualin** (25 miles, 190m) then descend

A small pedestrian ferry connects Keoldale with the minibus to Cape Wrath

CYCLING THE NORTH COAST 500

<small>Side road to Keoldale beside Kyle of Durness leads to a small ferry across the Kyle that provides access to the Cape Wrath peninsula.</small>

alongside river Dionard valley and follow this to reach sandy estuary of **Kyle of Durness**. ◄ Climb over low ridge and descend to **Durness** (35 miles, 40m) (accommodation, hostel, refreshments, camping) on N coast of Scotland where stage ends at T-junction beside war memorial L.

DURNESS

In contrast to the rocky moorland that surrounds it, Durness (pop 350) sits on an isolated outcrop of limestone with cultivated and pastoral fields providing a living for crofters. During World War II a large radar station was built in the village. Most of its concrete buildings are in ruins but some have found new uses including a youth hostel. Nearby Balnakeil was the site of another military base, this time a Cold War early warning station. Advances in technology soon made it redundant and it lay derelict before being taken over in 1964 by New Age settlers as a craft village. Nowadays businesses here

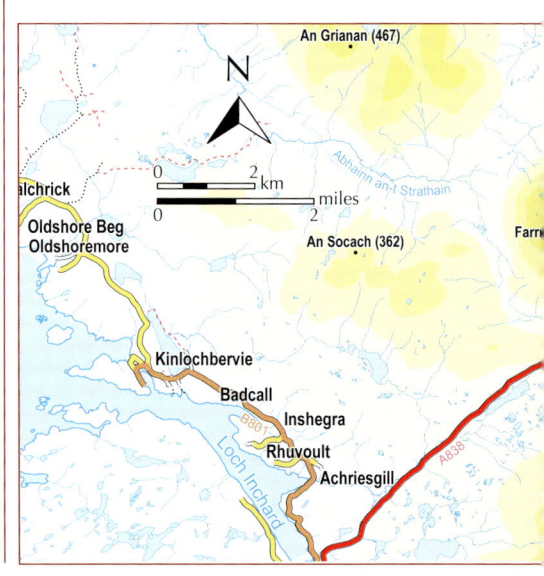

STAGE 8 – KYLESKU TO DURNESS

include a chocolate factory, art gallery and hairdresser. Durness is a base for excursions by ferry and minibus to Cape Wrath, the northwest extremity of mainland Britain with dramatic landscapes and the highest sea cliffs in the country. During his teenage years, John Lennon spent his summer holidays staying with cousins in Durness and a memorial garden in front of the village hall is dedicated to the former Beatle.

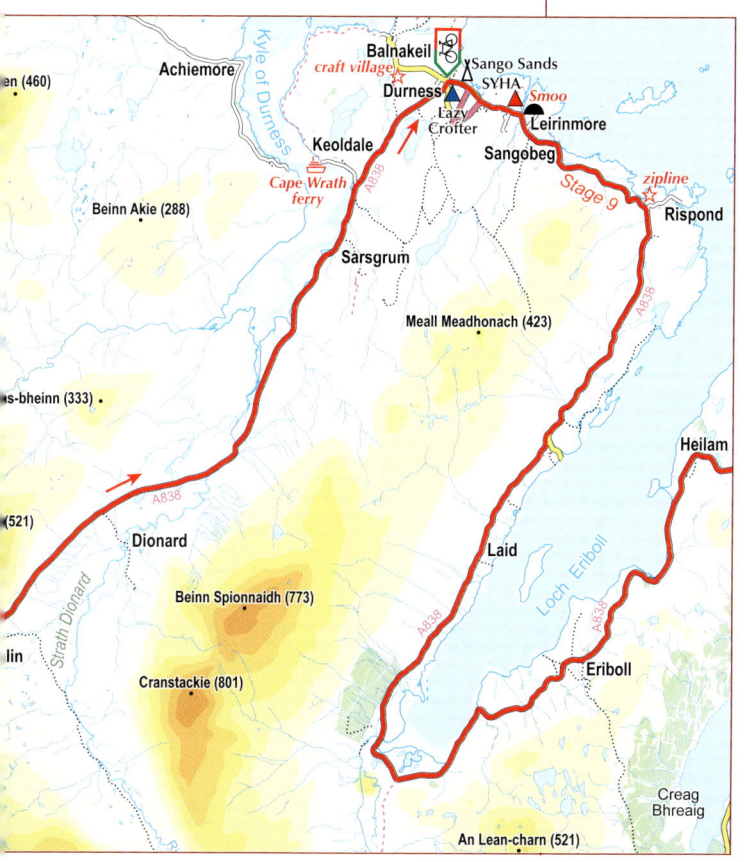

STAGE 9
Durness to Tongue

Start	Durness (40m)
Finish	Tongue, road junction (45m)
Distance	29.5 miles (47.5km)
Ascent	596m
Descent	591m
Waymarking	NC500 following A838

Now heading east along the top of Scotland, the route turns inland to pass round Loch Eriboll then crosses a large upland peat bog on the A'Mhoine plateau before descending to the MacKay seat of Tongue beside the Kyle of Tongue. Open country allows superb views both north over the coast and south to Ben Hope, the most northerly Munro.

From T-junction in **Durness**, follow A838 E and fork L on narrow road that drops down to cross Sango burn then rises very steeply to regain A838. Turn L and continue past village hall and John Lennon memorial garden (both R) into **Lerinmore** (1 mile, 32m) (accommodation, hostel, refreshments). Continue past entrance to **Smoo cave** L.

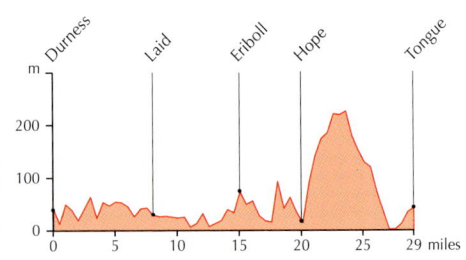

STAGE 9 – DURNESS TO TONGUE

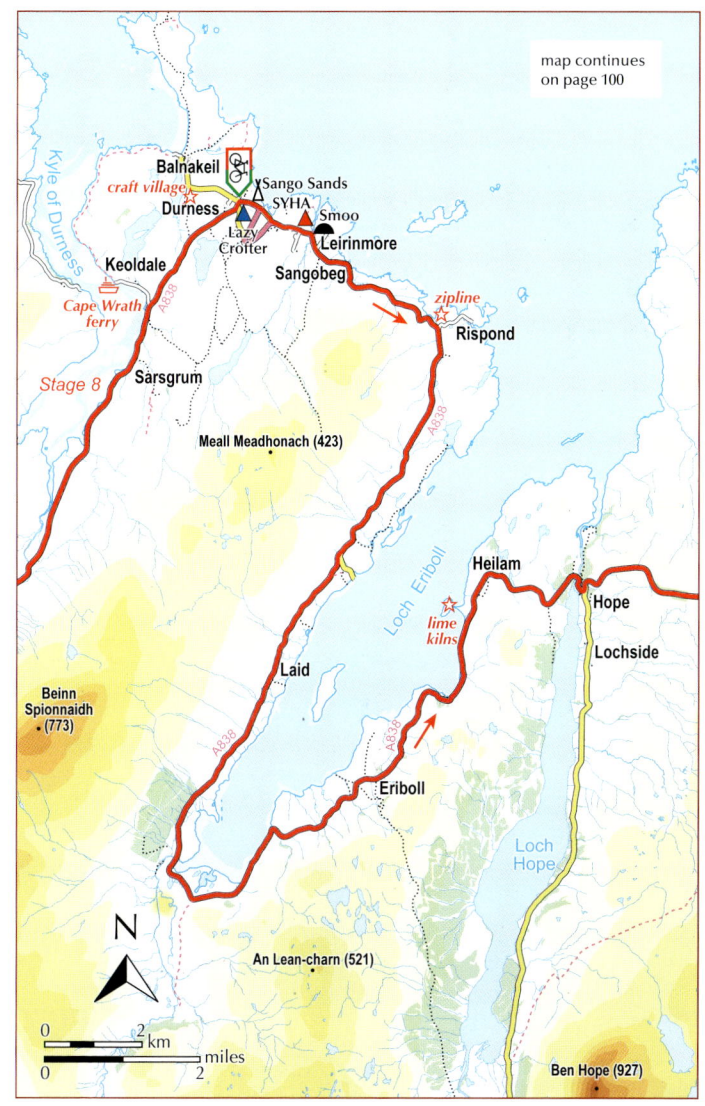

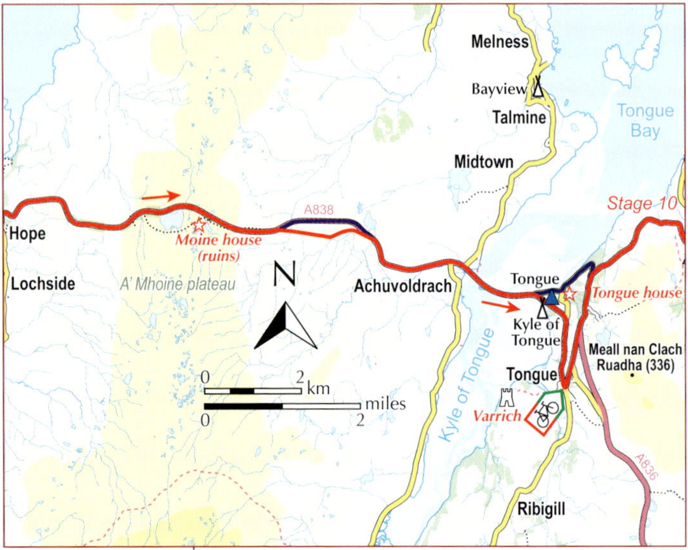

CYCLING THE NORTH COAST 500

Varrich castle stands on a hilltop overlooking the Kyle of Tongue

Smoo cave is unique within the UK being a combination of limestone sinkhole (cut from above by water seeping through the surface) and sea cave (cut from below by the action of waves) that have joined together underground. Inside the cave, the Alt Smoo river drops 20 metres over a waterfall between the two elements. Isostasis (post-glacial uplift) has raised the 40-metre-wide by 15-metre-high sea cave entrance above sea-level, making it accessible to visitors.

Continue parallel with coast through **Sangobeg** and pass Ceannabeinne beach. ▶ Follow road turning inland and contouring above cliffs beside W side of long narrow inlet of **Loch Eriboll** L and through spread out hamlet of **Laid** (8 miles, 40m) (accommodation, refreshments).

Loch Eriboll, which is 10 miles long and up to 120 metres deep, is used by ships as a safe anchorage during stormy weather. When *HMS Hood* anchored here in 1937, its crew picked out the

Smoo cave is entered from a sea inlet below Leirinmore

At Ceannabeinne, the Golden Eagle zipline connects high cliffs on either side of the bay travelling above the beach at 45mph.

ship's name in stones on the hillside overlooking the western side of the loch, a practice followed since by other ships. Navy crews in World War II nicknamed it Loch 'Orrible due to a lack of shore facilities.

> The disused lime quarry and kilns at Àrd Neakie previously burnt kelp to produce soda ash for use in glass and soap manufacture.

Descend to pass around head of loch and along its E side through **Eriboll**, another tiny hamlet. Climb away from loch passing unusually shaped Àrd Neakie peninsula below L. ◄ Continue over summit at Heilam (97m) and descend to cross **Hope bridge** (20 miles, 10m) at head of Loch Hope R.

Ascend very steeply (15 per cent) onto open moorland then continue across peat bogs of **A' Mhoine plateau**. Pass Loch Maovally R to reach summit (225m) by ruins of **Moine house**, with view of Ben Hope (927m) in distance R. Pass 'Parking ¼ mile' sign L and turn R to follow track across moorland on course of old road, rejoining main road after 1.2 miles. The track is suitable for hybrids and tourers: cyclists on racing bikes should stay on main road. Descend to cross long bridge/causeway across sand flats at mouth of **Kyle of Tongue** then follow road bearing R at end of causeway. ◄ Pass hostel L and continue with Ben Loyal rising beyond village to reach road junction in **Tongue** (29.5 miles, 45m) (accommodation, hostel, refreshments, camping).

> To bypass Tongue, fork L at end of causeway along seashore road, bear L past Tongue house R and ascend through woods to join main road on Stage 10, 1.5 miles beyond Tongue.

TONGUE

Tongue (pop 550) developed after the clearances as crofters evicted from the interior of Sutherland were resettled here. The 11th-century Varrich castle, the ruins of which stand on a hilltop west of the village overlooking the Kyle of Tongue, was the ancient stronghold of Clan MacKay. Later the clan seat moved to Tongue House (built 1670) near the mouth of the Kyle. Clan MacKay has a long history of giving military aid to the crown, supporting the royalists during the Civil War, the Hanoverians during the Jacobite uprisings of 1715 and 1745, providing troops for Wellington at Waterloo and fighting the Russians in Crimea. During the 1745 Jacobite rebellion, the Royal Navy chased a rebel ship into the Kyle. The ship was carrying French gold and

Ben Loyal (764m), rises just south of Tongue

supplies for the Stuarts. This was unloaded during the cover of darkness but once ashore the crew and cargo were captured by the MacKays. It is thought that this loss of gold may have contributed to Bonnie Prince Charlie's defeat at Culloden; it could have been used to pay for soldiers and equipment.

STAGE 10
Tongue to Melvich

Start	Tongue, road junction (45m)
Finish	Melvich, Halladale bridge (8m)
Distance	27.5 miles (44.5km)
Ascent	744m
Descent	781m
Waymarking	NC500 and Far North Way, following A836

This stage continues along the north coast, undulating over six small hills on open moorland and descending between them into valleys filled with the fields of small crofts and rivers that empty into the Pentland Firth.

From road junction in **Tongue**, follow A836 NE, joining Far North Way cycle route after end of village and ascend steadily through Tongue wood. Pass through Rhitongue (accommodation, refreshments) and **Coldbackie**, contouring across slopes of Ben Tongue R, then descend into **Strath Tongue** (3.5 miles, 70m).

Ascend over open moorland (summit 120m) winding past lochans, then descend past turn-off for **Borgie** (7 miles, 32m). ◄ Ascend over rocky ridge, passing summit (153m) at Lochan Leacach R, then descend into Strath Naver. Follow road bearing L parallel with river Naver,

Fork L to reach Borgie (accommodation, refreshments) after 500 metres.

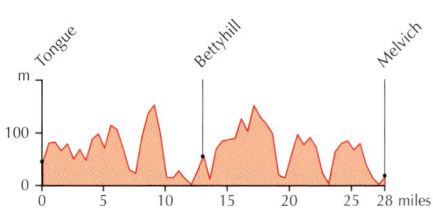

then cross river at **Invernaver** (accommodation) and ascend gently to **Bettyhill** (13 miles, 60m) (accommodation, refreshments, camping).

BETTYHILL

Bettyhill, which sits astride a headland between Torrisdale bay on the west and Farr bay on the east, is named after Elizabeth (Betty) Countess of Sutherland, wife of the first Duke. The village was established to accommodate crofters displaced from Strathnaver by the clearances of 1814. There was a salmon netting fishery below the village across the mouth of the river Naver equipped with a pier and ice house, although these are now disused. In Clachan, on the eastern edge of the village, the old parish church holds the Strathnaver museum with displays describing the clearances and a room dedicated to the history of Clan MacKay. The Farr stone in the churchyard is a large eighth-century Pictish cross carved with many symbols.

Descend into valley of Clachan Burn then ascend steadily onto rocky moorland to summit (155m). Follow road winding down Crasbackie hill to **Armadale** (19 miles 23m) (accommodation). Ascend again, over open

A new section of road takes the route over Cnoc an Rathaid Mhòir

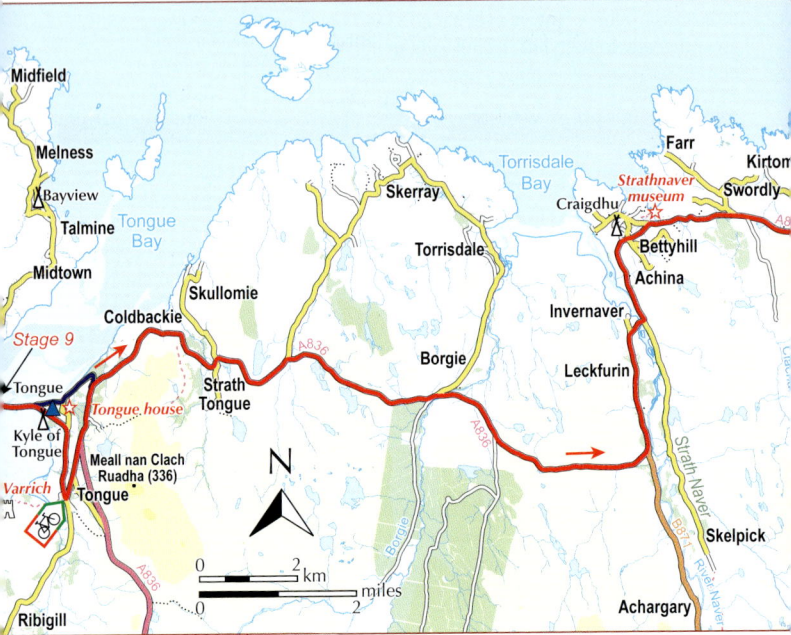

moorland of Cnoc an Rathaid Mhòir (summit 105m), then descend to cross river Strathy at **Strathy** (22.5 miles, 5m) (accommodation, refreshments).

Strathy is a small community of isolated residences that spreads for a mile along the main road, either side of Strathy bridge and north beside Strathy bay. It grew as a resettlement village after clearances began on the Strathy estate in 1790. Strathy Point lighthouse, which opened in 1958 at the end of a peninsula 2.5 miles north of the village, was the last manually operated lighthouse built in Britain.

Ascend over more open moorland (summit 84m) and descend through **Melvich** (26 miles, 56m) (accommodation, refreshments, camping) to reach **Halladale bridge**

STAGE 10 – TONGUE TO MELVICH

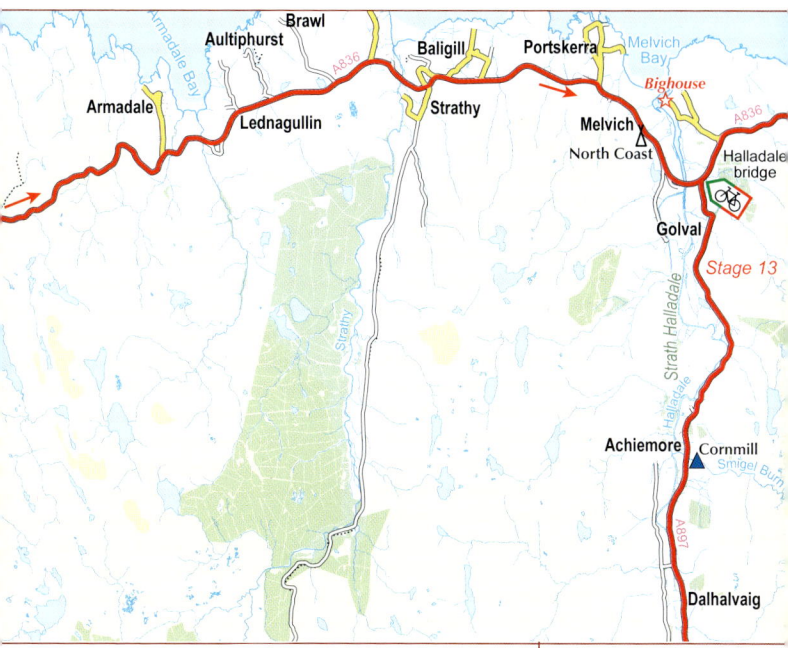

and stage end at A897 junction just E of bridge (27.5 miles, 8m).

Melvich is another spread out community occupying a strip of fertile land between the main road and the mouth of the river Halladale. Bighouse, formerly the principal residence of the leader of Clan MacKay, sits across the river mouth opposite the village. Nowadays used as a conference centre and upmarket shooting estate, it has a two-acre walled garden divided into four elements representing river, forest, valley and hill with metallic sculptures that reflect each theme. The garden is open to visitors one day each year, with profits going to the Royal National Lifeboat Institution.

After Melvich, the cycle route turns south (Stage 13) through the remote countryside of central Sutherland. Stages 11 and 12 allow a circular excursion to be made to visit John o' Groats before heading south. Stage 11 describes a route along the coast following the NC500 on quiet main roads while Stage 12 is a waymarked return journey on an inland route following Far North Way on asphalt surfaced country lanes. Both routes can be followed in either direction.

STAGE 11

*Melvich to John o' Groats
(coastal route)*

Start	Melvich, Halladale bridge (8m)
Finish	John o' Groats signpost (5m)
Distance	35.5 miles (57km)
Ascent	396m
Descent	399m
Waymarking	NC500, following A836

Quiet main roads are followed to visit the northeastern extremity of mainland Britain. A low ridge is crossed between Forss and Thurso but otherwise the stage is level or gently undulating across the pastoral landscape of Caithness. Thurso is the largest town encountered since leaving Inverness, giving you a chance to stock up on supplies or get adjustments made to your cycle.

From road junction at E end of **Halladale bridge**, follow A836 E (sp Thurso) ascending gently over scrubby moorland crossing from Sutherland into Caithness then descend to cross Sandside burn and continue past golf course L to **Reay** (5 miles, 12m). Pass turn-off for Shebster R and continue past **Dounreay** nuclear research station L (7 miles, 25m). ◄

Far North Way turns R to Shebster, the route followed by Stage 12 returning from John o' Groats.

STAGE 11 – MELVICH TO JOHN O'GROATS (COASTAL ROUTE)

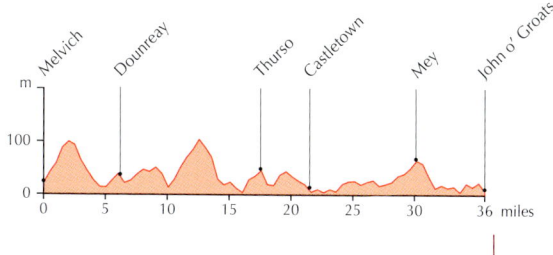

Prototype fast-breeder nuclear reactor at Dounreay

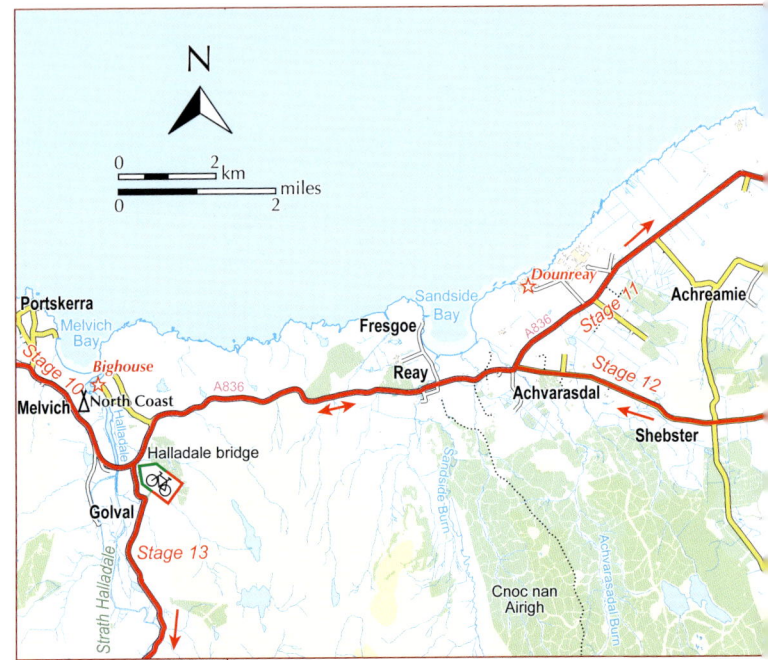

DOUNREAY

Dounreay was the site of a World War II airfield that was transferred to the Atomic Energy Authority in 1955 as a research station to investigate producing electricity using fast-breeder plutonium fuelled reactors. Three nuclear reactors were constructed, one to test materials, one to investigate the fast-breeder system and one as a prototype for commercial power stations. The first went online in 1958 and research continued until the prototype was shut down in 1998 when it was assessed that the fast-breeder system was not economically viable. Two further reactors that were used to test nuclear propulsion systems for submarines operated on a nearby site from 1970 to 2015. Decommissioning will take many years and it is projected that Dounreay will not be clear of radiation until the 2070s. If you want to see what it was like inside Dounreay, the North Coast Visitor Centre in Thurso has an exhibition which includes the control room from the reactor.

Stage 11 – Melvich to John o' Groats (coastal route)

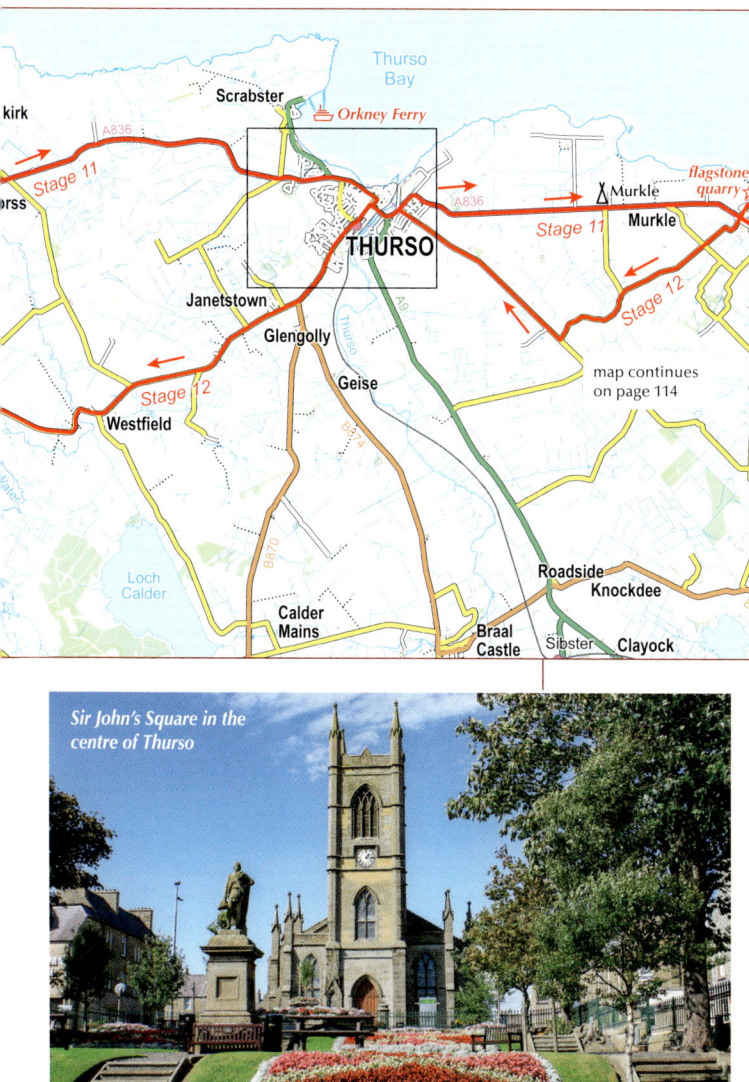

Sir John's Square in the centre of Thurso

Descend to cross Forss water and pass through **Forss** (10 miles, 17m) (accommodation, refreshments) then climb over low ridge (summit 101m) and descend past Thurso business park R and Burnside housing development L (accommodation, refreshments) to reach beginning of Thurso. Continue ahead (Olrig St) to T-junction and follow main road R (Traill St) to reach Sir John's Sq in centre of **Thurso** (15.5 miles, 10m) (accommodation, hostel, refreshments, camping, cycle shop, station).

THURSO

Thurso (pop 7400), which gets its name from the Norse god Thor, was an important Viking port, trading with Scandinavia and northern Europe, until Viking possessions in Scotland were ceded to the Scots in 1266 following defeat at the battle of Largs. The oldest building in town, the ruined 12th-century St Peter's church, dates from this time. Fishing, linen cloth production and leather tanning (Caithness is a cattle-rearing region) were the main industries in medieval times. Thurso participated in the 19th-century herring boom, its position enabling boats to catch fish off the east, north and west coasts of Scotland and land herring for processing and distribution by the Far North railway. The harbour was further expanded to ship flagstones cut from local sandstone for use as paving stones throughout the world. Much of the town centre was built during this period as a planned town on a grid layout. The herring and flagstone industries declined in the 20th century, reducing Thurso's prosperity until the Atomic Energy Authority arrived at Dounreay in 1955. Wick expanded with housing developments surrounding the old centre to accommodate many of the 2500 employees and their families brought in by the AEA. Although the reactors at Dounreay are no longer operational, many of the staff are still employed on nuclear clean-up programmes.

Turn L at traffic lights (Sir George's St, A9, sp John o' Groats) and cross bridge over river Thurso. Fork L at traffic lights (A836, sp Castletown) then follow road past Thurso East housing development R and bear R into open country. Pass through **Murkle** (accommodation, camping) and continue to **Castletown** (20.5 miles, 23m) (accommodation, refreshments).

Stage 11 – Melvich to John o' Groats (coastal route)

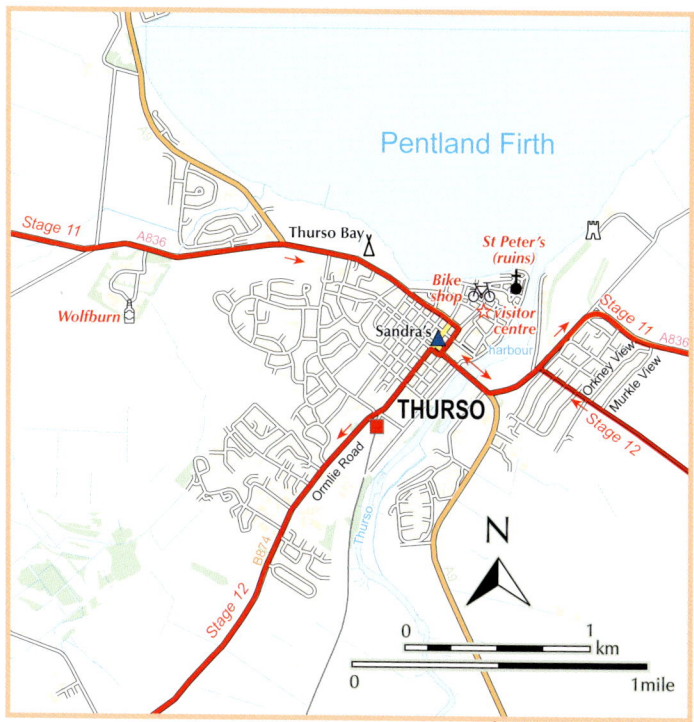

Cycle through town on Main St then bear L into open country. Pass behind dunes of Dunnet bay L and continue through **Dunnet** (24 miles, 20m) (accommodation, refreshments, camping). ▶ Pass Saint John's loch L and continue across open farmland to **Mey** (28.5 miles, 37m) (accommodation, refreshments).

CASTLE OF MEY

The 16th-century Castle of Mey, which sits in a position overlooking the Pentland Firth, is best known as the former Scottish summer residence of Queen Elizabeth the Queen Mother. During

Dunnet Head, 5 miles by road north of the route, is the most northerly point of mainland Britain. A lighthouse and viewpoint overlooking the Orkneys sits above 100m-high cliffs.

113

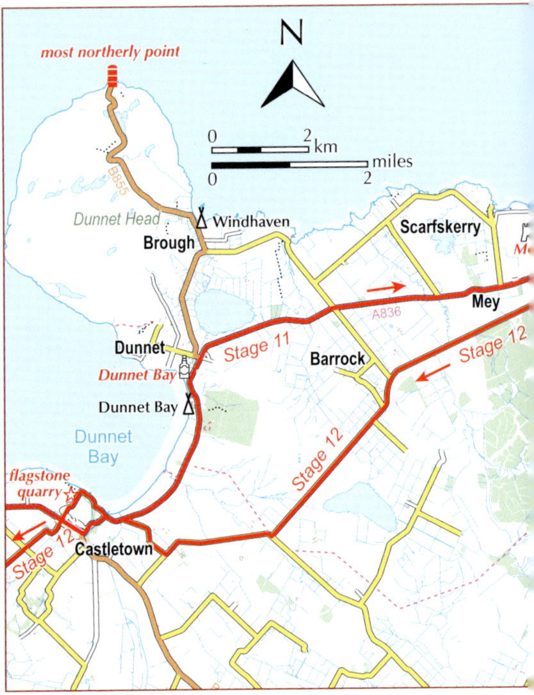

CYCLING THE NORTH COAST 500

nearly 400 years, the name changed to Barrogill castle as it passed through various hands with a number of additions and alterations to the original design. In 1952 it was bought in a semi-derelict state by The Queen Mother shortly after the death of King George VI. She reinstated the original name and removed

Stage 11 – Melvich to John o' Groats (coastal route)

some 19th-century additions. The interior was renovated and restored while outside beautiful gardens were created. The Queen Mother visited the castle every summer and was usually in residence when the Royal Yacht *Britannia* passed through the Pentland Firth taking the royal family to Balmoral for their annual summer visit to Scotland; salutes were exchanged between ship and shore. In 1996, ownership was passed to a charitable trust and this has continued to manage the property since the Queen Mother's death in 2002. The castle and gardens are open to visitors from mid-May until the end of September.

Follow road through **East Mey** (accommodation, hostel) and on to **Gills** (31 miles, 35m) (accommodation,

Gills has a small ferry port with regular car ferry sailings to Saint Margaret's Hope on the Orkney island of South Ronaldsway.

camping). ◄ Continue past **Canisbay church** L, where the Queen Mother used to attend services when she was in residence at Mey, and **Huna** to reach T-junction in front of Seaview hotel. Turn L (A99, sp John o' Groats) downhill to reach car park in **John o' Groats** (35.5 miles, 5m) (accommodation, refreshments, camping, tourist office) beside signpost showing 'Land's End 874 miles'.

JOHN O' GROATS

John o' Groats (pop 300) is often mistakenly described as the most northerly point in Britain. It is not (that is Dunnet Head, passed earlier), but it is the northern end of the longest possible journey between British settlements, being 874 miles from Land's End in southwest England. The name comes from a Dutchman Jan de Groot ('big John') who once operated the ferry to Orkney and who built a house overlooking the small harbour. The present-day village is not much to write home about, being a ramshackle collection of buildings at the end of the main road, indeed guidebooks variously describe it as a 'seedy tourist trap', a 'carbuncle' or even 'Scotland's most dismal village'. The most photographed sight is the signpost. From 1964 to 2013 this was a privately owned attraction where visitors paid a fee to be photographed beside the sign, changed to show the distance to their hometown. When a new hotel was built (2013) this was replaced with a public signpost displaying the distances to Land's End and other key destinations.

The signpost at John o' Groats shows 874 miles to Land's End

From John o' Groats the NC500 motorists' route turns south following the A99 and A9 roads to Tain. These are busy main roads with fast-moving traffic. The route following them is described in Stages 12A–14A. To avoid the traffic, a route recommended for cyclists is described here as Stages 12–14. This mostly follows the Far North Way, a part of National Cycle Network route 1 (NCN1) running south through the centre of Scotland to rejoin the motorists' route at Tain. To do so it is first necessary to return to Melvich using Stage 12 on an inland route different from Stage 11.

STAGE 12
John o' Groats to Melvich (inland route)

Start	John o' Groats signpost (5m)
Finish	Melvich, Halladale bridge (8m)
Distance	36.5 miles (58.5km)
Ascent	432m
Descent	429m
Waymarking	Far North Way
Note	For map see Stage 11

The return route from John o' Groats to Thurso and Melvich uses waymarked minor country lanes along a series of low ridges a little inland from the coastal route described in Stage 11. It drops down to pass through Castletown and Thurso but otherwise runs through a gently undulating landscape of fields and farms.

From **John o' Groats**, cycle S on A99 for 600 metres then turn R opposite Seaview hotel (A836, sp Thurso). Follow road through pastoral fields past **Huna** then turn L (sp Canisbay) and fork immediately R. Continue through **Canisbay** (3 miles, 40m) to reach T-junction. Turn R and continue through **Upper Gills**, with view R over Gills Bay and Pentland Firth to the distant Orkneys, on narrow road through fields and moorland. Continue past **Barrock** R and Inkstack L to reach T-junction (11.5 miles, 32m). Turn R (sp

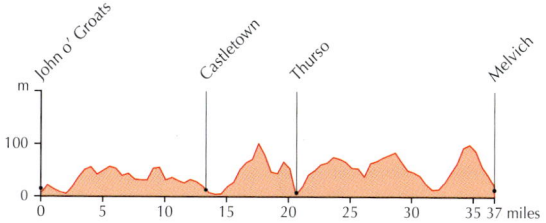

John o' Groats hotel overlooks the Pentland Firth

Castletown) then fork immediately L. Pass cottage R called 'The Chimneys' then turn R and continue past remnants of former military base to reach main road. Turn L (A836) and after 400 metres turn R (sp Castlehill heritage centre) opposite ruined mill. Pass small harbour R and bend L beside ruined quarry buildings that are now Castlehill heritage centre L. Continue into **Castletown** (14.5 miles, 23m) (accommodation, refreshments).

In 1824, James Traill began quarrying **flagstones** at Castlehill beside the Pentland Firth. The local old red sandstone was easily split into thin flat slabs ideal for cutting and dressing into paving 'flags'. The business grew rapidly with dressed stones exported through a purpose-built harbour to markets throughout the world. Caithness flags were used to pave The Strand in London, as well as streets in New York and Melbourne. The introduction of concrete paving stones at the end of the 19th century led to a collapse in the market for natural flagstone and the quarry closed in 1912.

Cross main road beside Castletown hotel R in middle of village and continue out of village, winding through fields. Go ahead over crossroads then pass large farm at

Sibminster and ascend over summit (102m), with old flagstone quarry L, to T-junction. Turn R (sp Thurso) and follow road descending through fields to Mount Pleasant housing development. Turn L at main road (A836 again) then bear R at traffic lights and cross river Thurso. Continue (Sir George's St) to reach traffic lights in Sir John's Sq in centre of **Thurso** (20.5 miles, 10m) (accommodation, hostel, refreshments, camping, cycle shop, station). ▶

Go ahead along L side of square and turn L beside Pentland hotel (Princes St, B874, sp Colaiste college). Bear R (Ormlie Rd) passing station L, then continue past high school and technical college (both L) and hospital R into open country. Keep ahead at road junction (sp Shebster) and continue past industrial area R at **Janetstown**. Follow road undulating gently and winding through **Westfield** (25 miles, 52m) (refreshments). Pass Baillie windfarm R and continue through **Shebster** (28 miles, 82m) before descending to reach main road. Turn L (A836 yet again!) and pass through **Reay** (31.5 miles, 12m. Cross Sandside burn then ascend over low ridge and descend to reach road junction on E side of **Halladale bridge** (36.5 miles, 8m) before **Melvich** (accommodation, refreshments in Melvich, camping).

The ruined windmill at Castlehill quarry was built of local flagstones

For map of Thurso see Stage 11.

STAGE 13
Melvich to Altnaharra

Start	Melvich, Halladale bridge (8m)
Finish	Altnaharra hotel (82m)
Distance	48.5 miles (78km)
Ascent	445m
Descent	371m
Waymarking	None, follow A897 Melvich–Kinbrace, B871 Kinbrace–Syre, B873 Syre–Altnaharra

This long stage starts by following a very quiet main road gently ascending Strath Halladale past remote crofts that survived early 19th-century land clearances (Strath Halladale was only partially cleared) to reach the flow country, a huge area of blanket peat bog. It then uses narrow moorland roads through wild desolate country with very little human habitation as the result of more aggressive clearances. The gradient undulates gently through valleys and over low rounded hills.

From road junction on E side of **Halladale bridge** near Melvich, follow A897 S beside river Halladale R. Pass small community of **Golval** and follow road undulating gently along Strath Halladale to reach **Achiemore** (4 miles, 30m) (hostel). Continue through **Dalhalvaig** and Beacrie, then follow road across river on Forsinain bridge (9 miles, 65m). Ascend gently along valley, now with river L to reach **Forsinard station** (14 miles, 154m) (accommodation, station).

FLOW COUNTRY

The river Halladale drains the flow country, a vast area of blanket peat bog that covers 1500 square miles of central Sutherland and Caithness. This peat has built up over many years from sphagnum moss growing in areas of poor drainage over impervious rock sub-strata. During the 1980s, a successful

STAGE 13 – MELVICH TO ALTNAHARRA

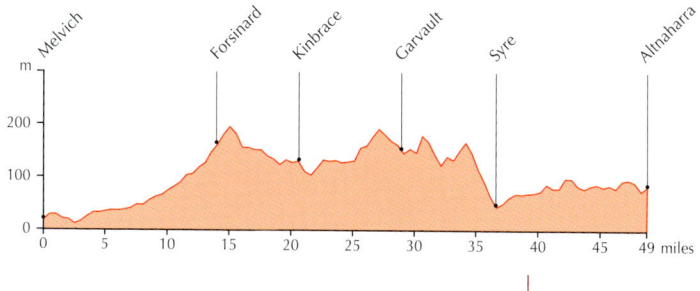

scheme to encourage investment in forestry by providing tax incentives to investors led to large areas being drained and planted with commercial conifer forests. Pressure from environmentalists led to this policy being abandoned in 1988 and as the trees reach maturity and are harvested the peat bog is being allowed to return. One particular organisation, the Royal Society for the Protection of Birds (RSPB), has purchased a number of estates around Forsinard and created a 25,000-acre nature reserve with a visitor centre at Forsinard and viewing tower overlooking Dubh lochan. A wide variety of birds can be seen on the moors and around the lochans, including dunlin, golden plover, hen harriers and greenshanks.

At Forsinard the RSPB have built a lookout to observe birds on their nature reserve

CYCLING THE NORTH COAST 500

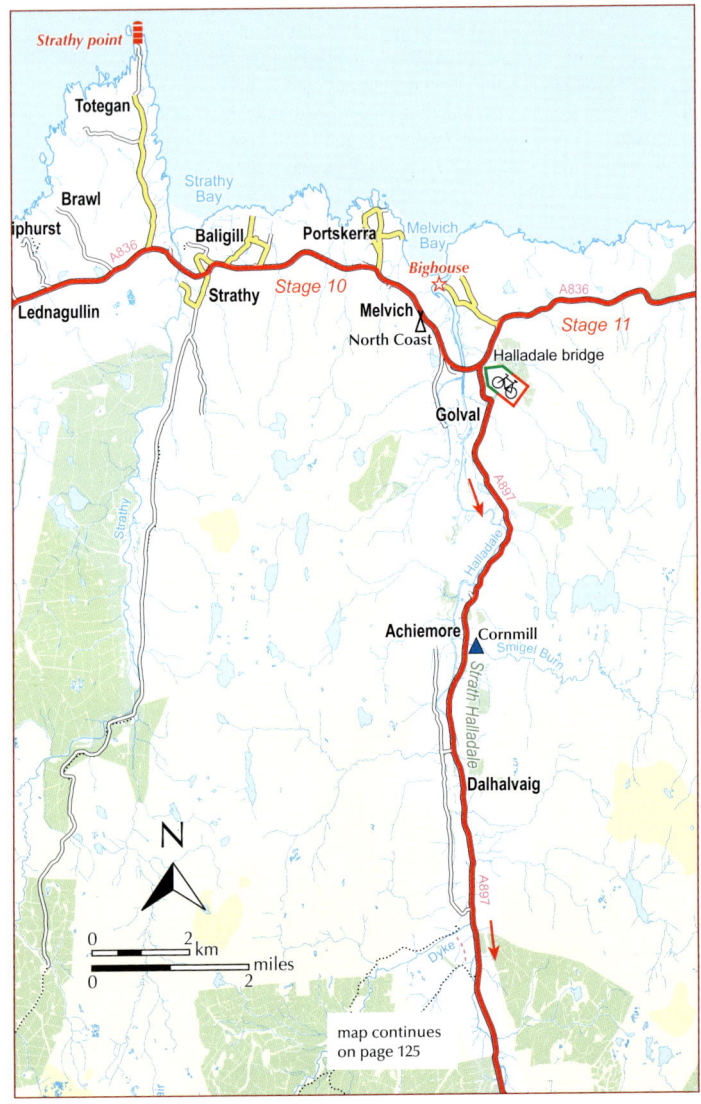

STAGE 13 – MELVICH TO ALTNAHARRA

Continue over railway crossing and climb gently across open moorland to unmarked summit (196m) at head of Strath Halladale. Descend equally gently into Strath Beg and continue descending parallel with railway R, passing between **Loch an Ruathair** R and small community of **Lochside** L, to reach **Kinbrace** (21 miles, 129m) (station).

Fork R (B871, sp Syre), descending to cross railway and pass station L. Continue over Bannoch Burn stream and follow road running parallel with river Helmsdale. Ascend gently up Strath Helmsdale passing Loch Achnamoine L and **Badanloch** sporting estate L (25.5 miles, 150m). Continue over summit (192m), then descend past Loch nan Clar L and **Garvault hotel** R (29 miles, 165m) (accommodation, refreshments). ▶ Road now undulates across open moorland with patches of forest L, then descends into Strath Naver. Cross bridge over river Naver to reach T-junction in **Syre** (36.5 miles, 50m).

Standing among thousands of acres of empty moorland, the Garvault hotel calls itself, justifiably, the most remote hotel in Britain.

The Garvault hotel is the most remote in Britain

Cycling the North Coast 500

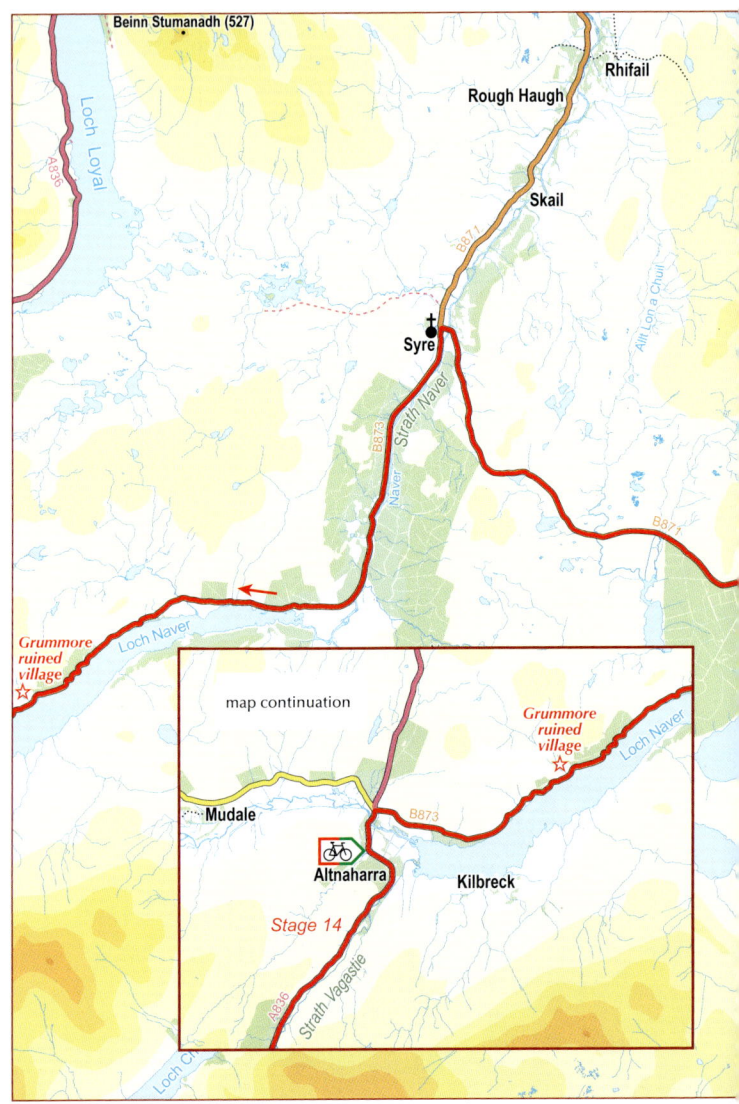

STAGE 13 – MELVICH TO ALTNAHARRA

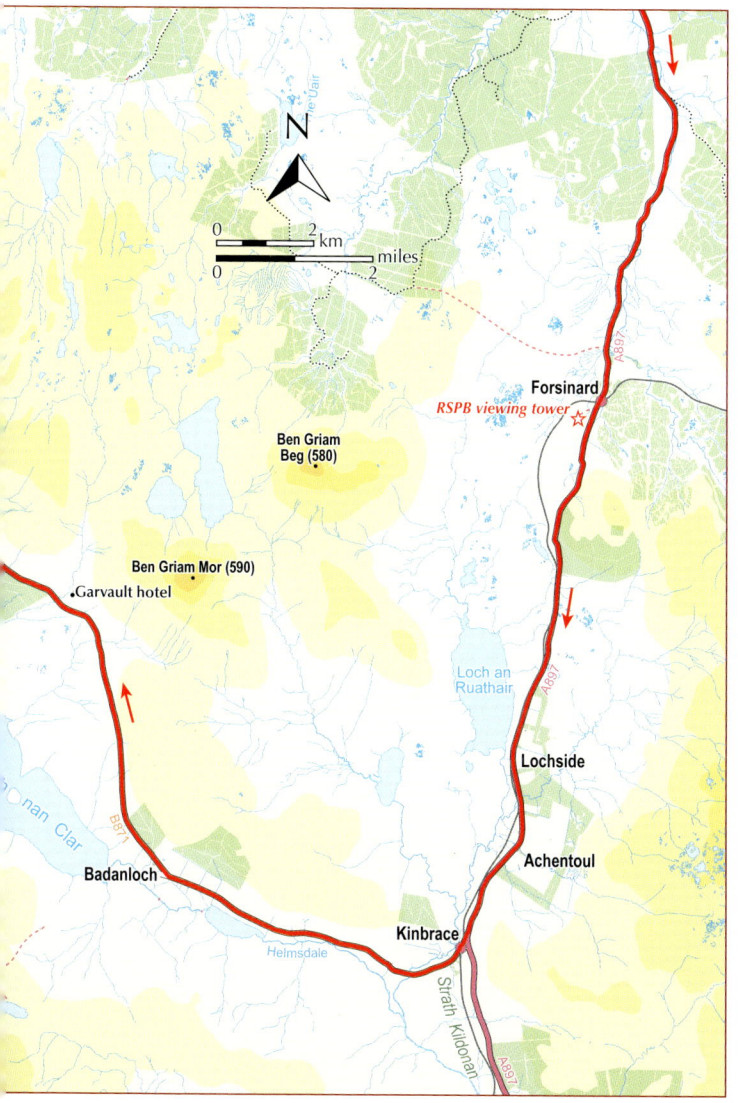

125

The 23-mile-long **Strath Naver** was the site of some of the most aggressive land clearances in the Highlands, carried out on behalf of the Duchess of Sutherland in the early 19th century. Whole villages were burnt to the ground and the crofters forced off the land. Most were relocated to coastal villages, some moved south to the Scottish industrial belt while others emigrated to North America and South Africa. Patrick Sellar, the factor who oversaw the clearances, was later prosecuted. The result was a transformation from subsistence agriculture to large-scale sheep farming. In the 20th century, part of this land was turned over to commercial forestry. The river Naver, which flows through the valley, is one of the best rivers in Scotland for wild Atlantic salmon.

> Grummore was the first crofting village in Strath Naver cleared in 1814.

Turn L (B873, sp Altnaharra) and follow road parallel with river Naver L through forest. Continue alongside Loch Naver, passing site of cleared village at Grummore (45 miles, 80m) R to reach crossroads. ◄ Turn L (A836, sp Lairg) and cross bridge over river Mudale into **Altnaharra** (48.5 miles, 82m) (accommodation, refreshments) where stage ends by hotel.

The small hamlet of **Altnaharra** has the unenviable distinction of holding the record for the lowest recorded UK temperature, -27.2°C on 30 December 1995. Despite this, it is popular with anglers, stalkers and mountain walkers. Ben Klibreck (962m) rises south of the hamlet.

STAGE 14
Altnaharra to Tain

Start	Altnaharra hotel (82m)
Finish	Tain, tollbooth (27m)
Distance	46.5 miles (75km)
Ascent	299m
Descent	354m
Waymarking	Far North Way, following A836

A stage of two distinct parts: first a ride through wild moorland over the Crask pass and a descent through forest to Lairg, then a gentler trip through the valley of the river Shin to Tain on the shore of the Kyle of Sutherland. Quiet country roads are followed throughout with a gentle ascent for the first 7 miles, then it's downhill or level for the rest of the way.

From **Altnaharra**, follow A836 S, ascending steadily up Strath Vagastie beside river Vagastie L. Cross river at Vagastie bridge and continue across open moorland to soon reach summit (264m). Descend slightly to reach **Crask Inn** (7.5 miles, 230m) (accommodation, refreshments) at head of Strath Tirry. ▶ Continue ahead, contouring through forest, much of which has been felled, then descend over **Rhian** bridge and continue downhill beside river Tirry R to reach Loch Shin at **Dalchork** (17.5 miles, 109m) (camping). Follow lochside road past

The Crask was gifted by its previous owners to the Scottish Episcopal church. It still operates as an inn, with occasional religious services in the bar.

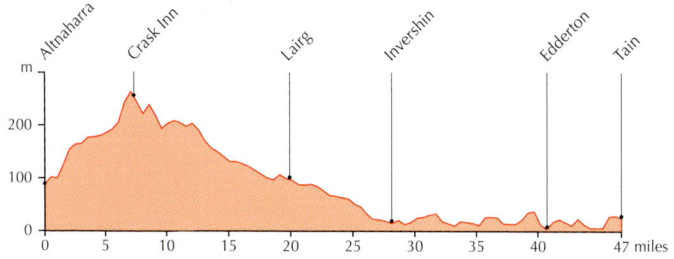

CYCLING THE NORTH COAST 500

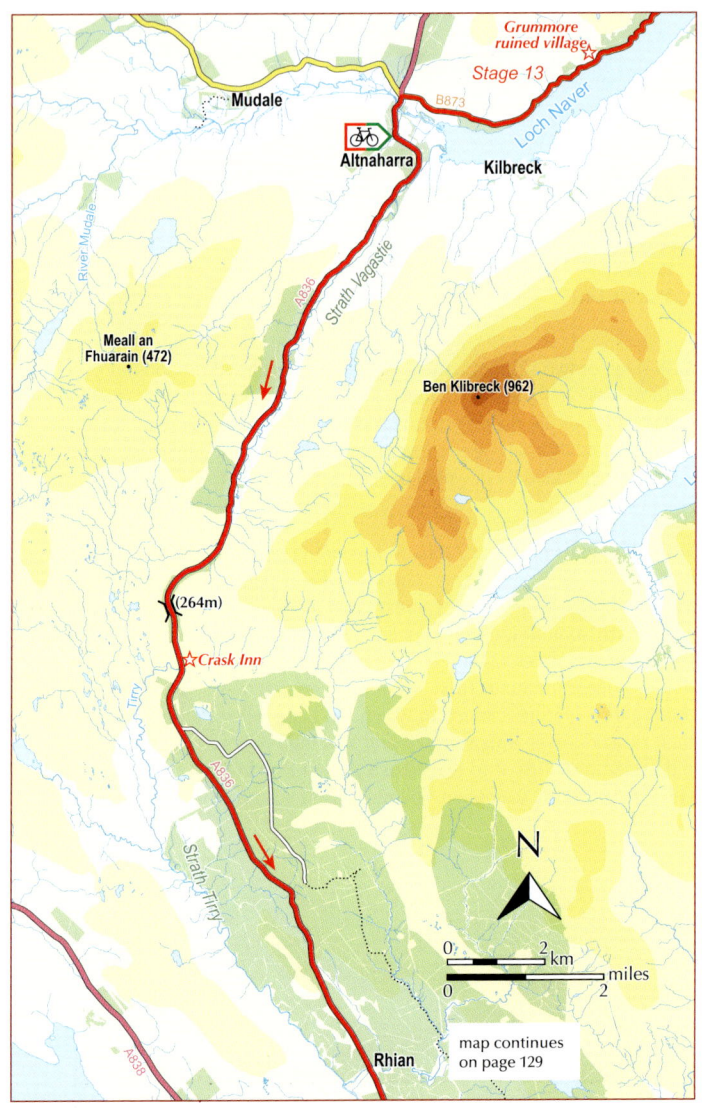

STAGE 14 – ALTNAHARRA TO TAIN

hydro-electric dam R and continue beside Little Loch Shin through **Lairg** (20.5 miles, 85m) (accommodation, refreshments, station). ▶

To reach town centre, turn L into Main St.

Lairg (pop 900) sits beside Little Loch Shin. With a network of roads radiating north and west through the hills and a nearby station on the Far North railway, it acts as a hub for communities across Sutherland with the title 'crossroads of the north'. The annual sheep market, held in August, claims to be the largest one-day sheep sale in Europe.

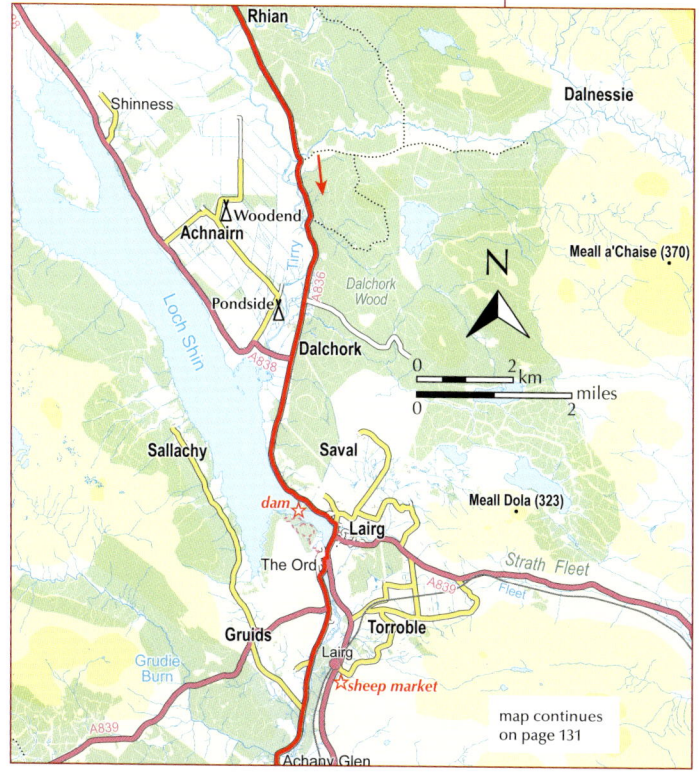

map continues on page 131

After end of built-up area, turn R on bridge over river Shin (A839, sp Ullapool) into **The Ord** then bear L beside river. Where road turns R away from river, fork L (B864, sp Invershin) to continue beside river. Cross bridge over Grudie Burn at head of Strath Grudie then continue descending gently through Shin forest past the **Falls of Shin** L (25 miles, 45m).

FALLS OF SHIN

Falls of Shin visitor centre

The Falls of Shin are a popular tourist sight. Although not very high, there is an impressive flow of water over the falls. The main attraction is the opportunity to watch salmon leaping the torrent, seen from May until late autumn and at its height in mid September. The falls were previously owned by former Harrods' proprietor Mohamed Al-Fayed, with a visitor centre that included a small branch of Harrods and a waxwork of Al-Fayed. After this centre was destroyed by fire, the falls were acquired by a community trust and a new visitor centre was built. Unfortunately the visitor centre and café proved to be commercially unviable and have remained closed since 2020.

Follow road beside river to reach road junction and turn L (A837) over river on Shin bridge. Continue to next T-junction and turn R (A836, sp Bonar Bridge) to reach **Invershin** (28 miles, 10m) (accommodation, hostel, refreshments, station).

The waymarked route uses 50 steps to climb up to and cross the river Shin using Invershin railway bridge. These steps can be avoided by staying on the A836 main road to **Bonar Bridge** (31.5 miles, 7m) (accommodation, refreshments, cycle shop, station), then turning R over river Shin (still A836) to re-join waymarked route in Ardgay.

STAGE 14 – ALTNAHARRA TO TAIN

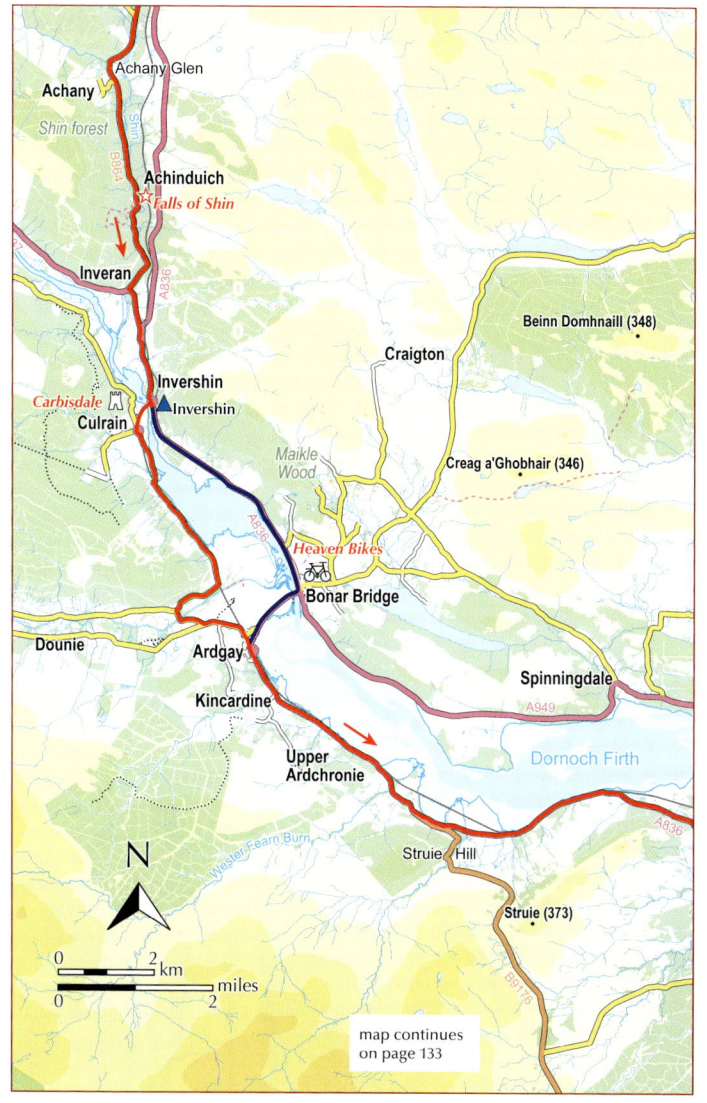

CARBISDALE CASTLE

Erected between 1906 and 17, Carbisdale was the last castle built in Scotland. It was built as a residence for Mary, Dowager Duchess of Sutherland after the death of her husband, the third Duke. His family had disapproved of the marriage and contested his will. Matters were settled by agreeing to give the Duchess a sum of money and promising to build her a castle. She chose the site at Culrain in Ross-shire because it overlooked Sutherland on the opposite side of the river. The clocktower has only three faces with a blank side towards Sutherland as she swore that she would never give the Sutherland family the time of day and the castle has become known as the 'castle of spite'. After her death, Carbisdale was bought by the Salvesens, a wealthy Edinburgh shipping family of Norwegian extraction, and used during World War II to house the King of Norway after the German invasion of his country. In 1945 it was gifted to the Scottish Youth Hostel Association and operated as a very eccentric hostel until 2011 when it closed for repairs. Extensive frost and water damage were discovered and the castle was subsequently offered for sale with the expectation that it would be converted into a luxury hotel or an exclusive private residence.

The bridge has steps with a ramp for pushing cycles and cycle track beside railway.

Pass under railway bridge and turn R opposite hotel onto combined cycle track/footpath that heads back under railway. Follow this L across Invershin bridge over river Shin, with **Carbisdale castle** R standing high above river on opposite bank. ◄

Continue on gravel track beside railway and bear L on road, passing **Culrain** station L (station). Cross bridge

The cycle route crosses Invershin bridge beside the Far North railway

STAGE 14 – ALTNAHARRA TO TAIN

over railway and continue between Kyle of Sutherland estuary L and railway R, soon passing back under railway bridge. Follow road beside railway, eventually bearing R with Invercharron House behind trees L to reach T-junction. Turn L (sp Ardgay) over river Carron then L again at next T-junction and follow road (Church St) to reach T-junction in **Ardgay** (32.5 miles, 4m).

Turn R (A836, sp Tain) passing entrance to station L. Continue beside railway and Kyle of Sutherland estuary (both L) past **Kincardine** hamlet and Wester Fearn. At **Struie** hill, where road forks, keep L (A836, sp Tain) and continue to **Edderton** (41 miles, 23m) (accommodation, station). ▶

Cycle through village and continue parallel with railway and estuary to Meikle Ferry roundabout at S end of Dornoch bridge (refreshments, camping). Go ahead over roundabout (A9, second exit, sp Tain using hard shoulder L as cycle lane) and pass Glenmorangie distillery L.

Balblair distillery in Edderton, which produces a range of vintage single malt whisky, has a visitor centre and distillery shop.

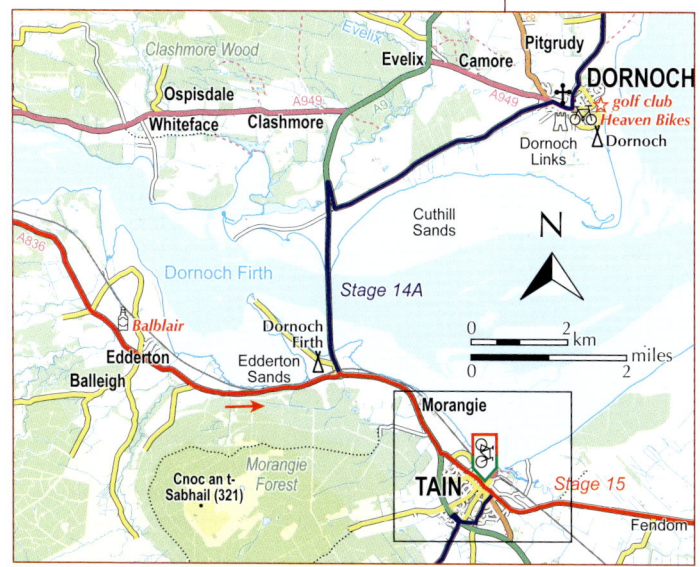

Glenmorangie distillery near Tain has the tallest stills in Scotland

Glenmorangie is the largest-selling single malt whisky in Scotland and the 10 million bottles produced annually give it a six per cent share of the world market. Distilling started in 1843 using two second-hand gin stills. The operation remained small scale until after World War II; indeed, the distillery was mothballed on a number of occasions between 1920–50 due to American prohibition, economic depression and the effects of war. Steady expansion since 1977 has seen 10 extra stills installed, the tallest stills in Scotland. In 2004 the company was bought by French luxury goods manufacturer LVMH (Louis Vuitton Moët Hennessy) who have introduced new products aimed at the world market for luxury goods.

Fork L (Morangie Rd, B9174, sp Tain industrial estate) and follow road becoming Academy Rd then Tower St to reach tollbooth clocktower L in centre of **Tain** (46.5 miles, 27m) (accommodation, refreshments, station).

STAGE 14 – ALTNAHARRA TO TAIN

TAIN

Tain (pop 3600) grew up around the birthplace of Saint Duthac (1000–1065), an early Christian missionary. It was granted a charter as a royal burgh in 1066, making Tain Scotland's oldest burgh. The charter gave the town rights as a sanctuary where fugitives could seek safety, a facility used by Robert the Bruce who sent his family to Tain when things were going badly during the First War of Scottish Independence (1296–1328). Later Saint Duthac's chapel became a place of pilgrimage when tales circulated about miracles surrounding the saint's relics. James IV (1473–1513) visited regularly, seeking to assuage the guilt he felt for his part in his father's death. Notable buildings include the tollbooth with its clocktower and the Pilgrimage, an old collegiate church (built 1370) that has been deconsecrated and is used for weddings and concerts although it has kept many of the architectural elements it had as a place of worship.

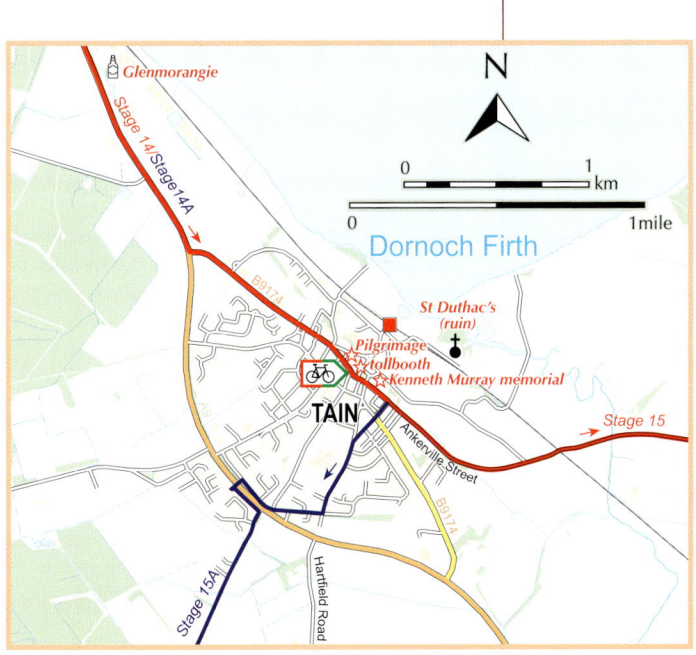

STAGE 12A
John o' Groats to Lybster

Start	John o' Groats harbour (5m)
Finish	Lybster crossroads (68m)
Distance	30 miles (48.5km)
Ascent	345m
Descent	282m
Waymarking	NC500, following A99

Turning south following the east coast, this stage follows the A99 through the pastoral cattle- and sheep-rearing countryside of northeast Sutherland, mostly contouring through fields above low sea cliffs. There are gentle ascents over two low moors with a descent between them to pass through Wick, the old county town of Sutherland.

From harbour in **John o' Groats**, follow A99 S past village. Ascend steadily through open moorland over shoulder of **Warth hill** (2.5 miles, 98m) then descend through treeless pastoral landscape of isolated farms in **Freswick** to **Auckengill** (6.5 miles, 33m) (accommodation). Continue, with sea 250m L beneath low cliffs, past **Keiss** castle house L (now a private residence) and Kirk Tofts broch

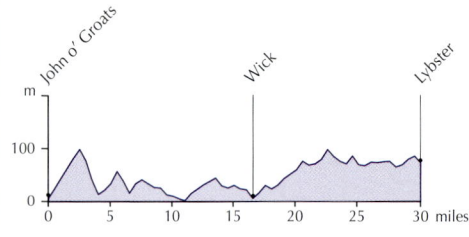

STAGE 12A – JOHN O' GROATS TO LYBSTER

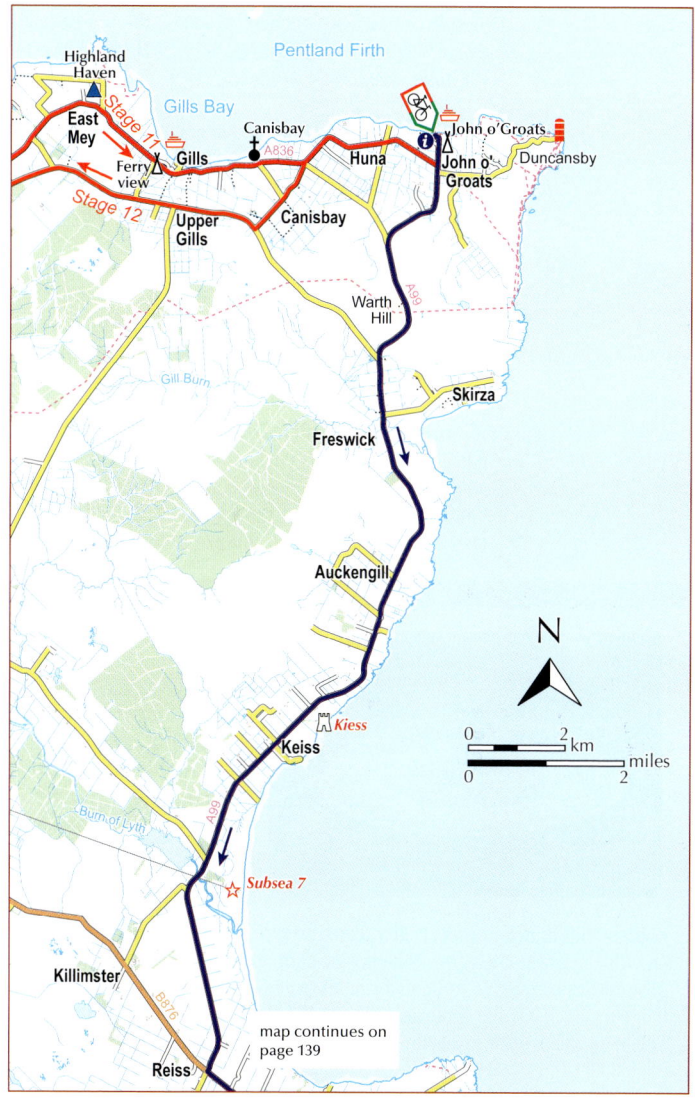

(beside cemetery R) into **Keiss** (8 miles, 28m) (accommodation, refreshments). Continue to reach Bridge of Wester (11 miles, 3m).

Bridge of Wester is the site of one of the strangest shaped manufacturing sites in Britain. The **Subsea 7** construction site is a slipway 7000 metres long by 15 metres wide. On this site, undersea pipelines are welded together before being towed out to connect oil wells beneath the North Sea. The site is wide enough to fabricate four pipes at a time, giving the site an ability to despatch pipelines in 27km (17.5 mile) lengths. An industrial railway connects the fabrication sheds at each end of this slipway.

Follow road ahead to T-junction in **Reiss** (13.5 miles, 42m). Turn L (A99, sp Wick) and continue past **Ackergill** and Wick airport L. Cycle ahead on George St to reach traffic lights in centre of **Wick** (16.5 miles, 8m) (accommodation, refreshments, camping, cycle shop, station).

WICK

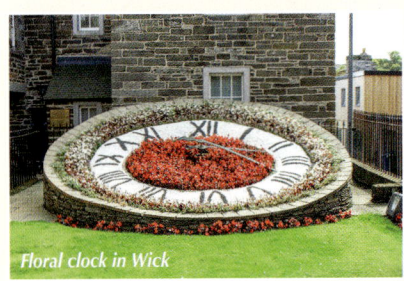
Floral clock in Wick

The natural harbour at Wick (pop 6900) was attractive to the Vikings who in the 11th century built a castle on the cliffs south of the harbour mouth. However, the town was slow to develop and by the early 18th century was still little more than a few stone houses with thatched roofs and a plank bridge over the river. Stimulus to growth came with the early 19th-century herring boom. Like Thurso, Wick's position was attractive to boats from all over northern Scotland, enabling them to reach fishing grounds off west, north and east coasts. Between 1803–11 the British Fisheries Society built the harbour and developed

STAGE 12A – JOHN O' GROATS TO LYBSTER

Pulteneytown, south of the river, with an area (lower town) for processing the fish and upper town as a residential district for fishermen and their families, many of them dispossessed crofters who had been evicted during the clearances. As a result, the harbour became, for a short time, the busiest fishing port in the world. The fish was processed and packed into barrels for export, mostly to the Baltic. Wick, north of the river, grew to provide commercial support with substantial stone houses, shops and offices. A bridge was built connecting the two communities which did not officially merge until 1902. When Old Pulteney distillery was opened in 1826 its barley was imported by sea and its whisky left the same way. Nowadays its range of single malts are transported by road. The water, however, still comes from its historic source in Loch Hempriggs.

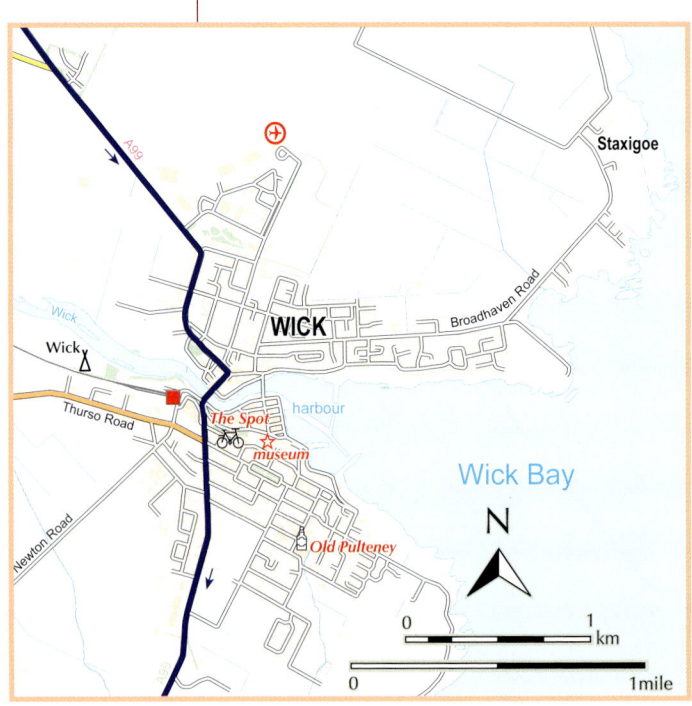

STAGE 12A – JOHN O' GROATS TO LYBSTER

Turn R (Bridge St) and follow road over river Wick. Go ahead (Cliff Rd) at mini-roundabout, uphill past hospital R. ▶ Keep ahead at traffic lights (Francis St, A99, sp Inverness) and continue on South St into open country. Cycle gently uphill past Loch Hempriggs R and continue through **Thrumster** (20.5 miles, 74m) (accommodation, refreshments). Pass summit (98m) on shoulder of Hill of Ulbster then descend slightly passing turn L for **Whaligoe steps**. Follow road contouring through spread out hamlet of **Mid Clyth** (24 miles, 71m) and **Occumster** (28.5km, 73m) (accommodation) to reach crossroads in **Lybster** (30 miles, 68m) (accommodation, refreshments).

To the left of the roundabout, 2-metre-long Ebenezer Place is in the Guinness Book of Records as the world's shortest street.

At Whaligoe, 365 steps cut into the cliffs lead down to a small natural harbour that once was home to 20 herring boats

STAGE 13A
Lybster to Brora

Start	Lybster crossroads (68m)
Finish	Brora clocktower (11m)
Distance	33 miles (53km)
Ascent	618m
Descent	675m
Waymarking	NC500, following A99 (Lybster–Latheron) then A9 (Latheron–Brora)

Continuing to follow the east coast and soon joining the A9 main road, this stage ascends twice from sea level to run above high sea cliffs, dropping back to sea level after both climbs. The landscape is mostly pastoral farmland on the seaward side of the route with rolling moorland inland. The road previously undulated and wound considerably more than it does now. New sections of road have removed much of this variation and bypassed the centres of Dunbeath and Helmsdale.

From crossroads in **Lybster** follow A99 S past **Forse** (accommodation) and continue to **Latheron** (3.5 miles, 86m). Follow main road bearing L and joining A9 (sp Inverness) to reach **Latheronwheel** (4.5 miles, 64m)

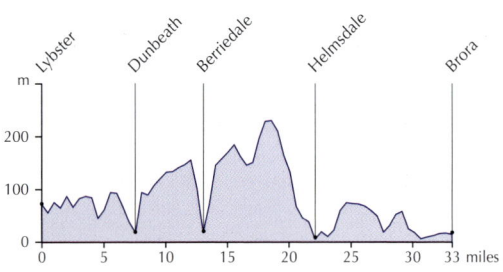

(accommodation) then continue past Croft museum in **Laidhay** L (refreshments).

At Laidhay an **18th-century longhouse croft** that remained occupied until 1968 has been preserved. Made of stone under a thatched roof, it is whitewashed inside and out with red doors and window frames. Inside is a collection of bric-a-brac. Humans and their animals all lived together in the house with a byre at the east end for the cattle. A cobbled trough in the middle of the byre took away liquid waste while a hatch in the end wall was used to dispose of manure.

Stay on main road to **Dunbeath** (7 miles, 25m) (accommodation, refreshments, camping). ▶ Cross new bridge and ascend steeply through **Balnabruich**. Continue climbing, now less steeply, to reach summit (154m) on shoulder of **Beinn nan Coireag** R, with high sea cliffs L. Descend steeply around two hairpin bends into coombe to cross Berriedale water in **Berriedale** (13 miles, 10m) (refreshments). Ascend steeply, with forest R, onto open

The preserved thatched croft at Laidhay museum is a typical 18th-century dwelling

In Dunbeath, the old road that previously dropped down to cross Dunbeath Water has been bypassed by a new high-level bridge.

CYCLING THE NORTH COAST 500

> To reach centre of village, turn R (Dunrobin St) beside Belgrave Arms hotel.

moorland and continue climbing to summit (18 miles, 230m) on slopes of Creag Thoraraidh R. Follow road downhill past **Navidale** (accommodation) to roundabout in **East Helmsdale**. Go ahead (A9, first exit, sp Helmsdale), then fork L beside hostel, following Stafford St into **Helmsdale** (22 miles, 10m) (accommodation, hostel, refreshments, station). ◄

Helmsdale (pop 700) stands beside a bridge over the river Helmsdale built in 1811 by Thomas Telford. In 1814, the Duke of Sutherland chose this site to build a planned community for evicted crofters and provide them with employment in the

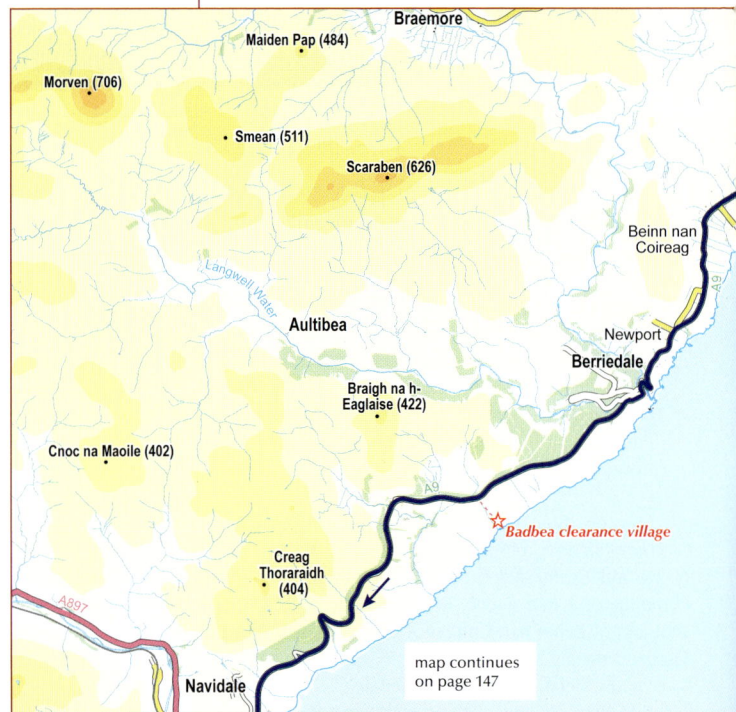

STAGE 13A – LYBSTER TO BRORA

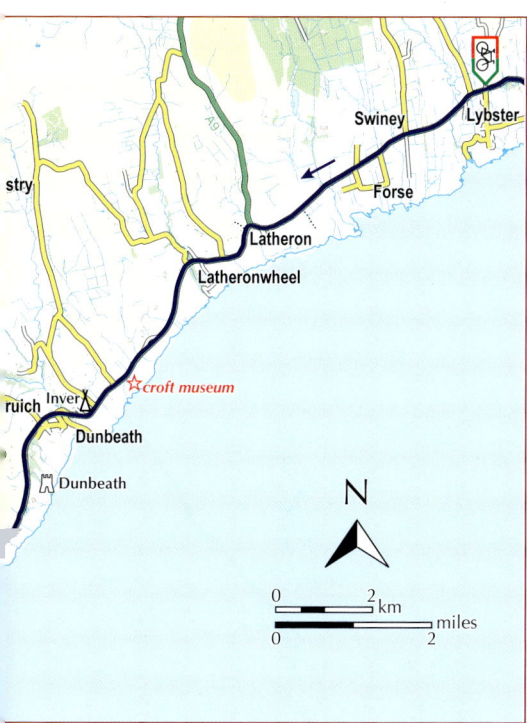

herring industry. Since the 1970s' construction of a high-level bridge, taking the A9 over the river, the village centre has become a quiet and sleepy place away from traffic. Beside the main road, just south of the new bridge, is a monument commemorating crofters who emigrated after being evicted from nearby Strath Kildonan between 1813–19 when 1574 residents were reduced to 257 by aggressive clearances. Many moved to Helmsdale but others went overseas to America, Canada, Australia and New Zealand with flags from these nations flying over the monument. In Canada, emigrants from Kildonan are credited with establishing Winnipeg.

Turning right after Dalchalm leads to the Clynelish and Brora distilleries.

Continue over river Helmsdale with view of harbour below L and pass emigrants memorial and visitor centre above road R. Cross railway bridge then follow road just above beach parallel with railway L with cliffs rising R. Bear R away from coast steeply uphill through **Portgower** (23.5 miles, 45m) (accommodation). Continue with fields L and moorland R through **Culgower** (26 miles, 70m) and descend through **Lothmore** (28 miles, 30m). Return briefly to coast then cycle through Greenhill and pass **Dalchalm** L (32 miles, 13m) (camping). ◄ Continue

STAGE 13A – LYBSTER TO BRORA

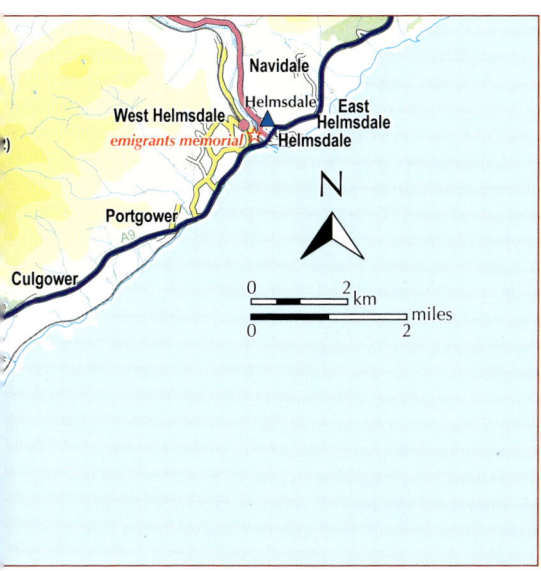

ahead on A9 (Victoria Rd) past station L and over river Brora to reach war memorial clocktower in **Brora** (33 miles, 11m) (accommodation, refreshments, station).

Brora (pop 1200) is a small post-industrial community with a coal mine that, before it closed in 1974, was the most northerly coal mine in Scotland. Originally the coal was used to heat salt pans that produced sea salt for use in processing the herring catch. A local stone quarry shipped architectural-quality limestone south to build structures as diverse as the new London bridge and Liverpool cathedral as well as nearby Dunrobin castle. There are two distilleries: Clynelish, which mostly produces blending whisky for use in Johnnie Walker gold label reserve, and Brora, which reopened in 2021 after being mothballed for many years.

STAGE 14A
Brora to Tain

Start	Brora clocktower (11m)
Finish	Tain, tollbooth (27m)
Distance	25 miles (40km)
Ascent	229m
Descent	213m
Waymarking	NC500, following A9 Brora–Golspie and from The Mound–Tain

After first undulating gently along the coast past Dunrobin castle, stately home of the Dukes of Sutherland, the route turns inland at Golspie to circle the flat lands bordering the Loch Fleet estuary and visit Dornoch, the old county town of Sutherland. After crossing a long bridge over the Dornoch Firth, the route joins Stage 14 to reach stage end in Tain.

From war memorial clocktower in **Brora** cycle S on Rosslyn St. Continue out of town parallel to railway through fields with low sea cliffs beyond. Pass ruins of **Carn Liath broch** L and follow road between entrance of **Dunrobin castle** L and station R (4.5 miles, 55m) (refreshments, station).

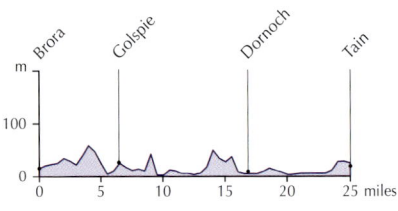

DUNROBIN CASTLE

Dunrobin castle is the ancestral home of the Dukes of Sutherland

The castle you can see at Dunrobin was built (1835–50) for the second Duke of Sutherland by Sir Charles Barry, the leading architect of the time following his rebuilding of the London Houses of Parliament. The building was designed to blend harmoniously with retained parts of an earlier castle on the site, particularly the 14th-century tower. The resulting castle is a mix of Scottish baronial and French château styles. With 189 rooms it is the largest castle in northern Scotland. A fire in 1915 destroyed much of the interior, leading to restoration by Sir Robert Lorimer. Interior decoration includes wood carvings by Grinling Gibbons, Chippendale furniture, and paintings by Canaletto and Reynolds. After the fifth duke died (1963) the castle became a boys' boarding school from 1965–72. Subsequently the castle and gardens were opened to the public, with part retained for private use by the Sutherland family. The nearby station on the Far North railway was a private station for the Sutherlands and their visitors. It is now open for use by all, but trains call only in summer. On Ben Bhraggie hill, southwest of Golspie, an enormous (30m-high) statue of the first duke dominates the view from all around. Objectors to the duke's involvement in the clearances have tried several times to topple the statue, but it has been repaired and still stands tall.

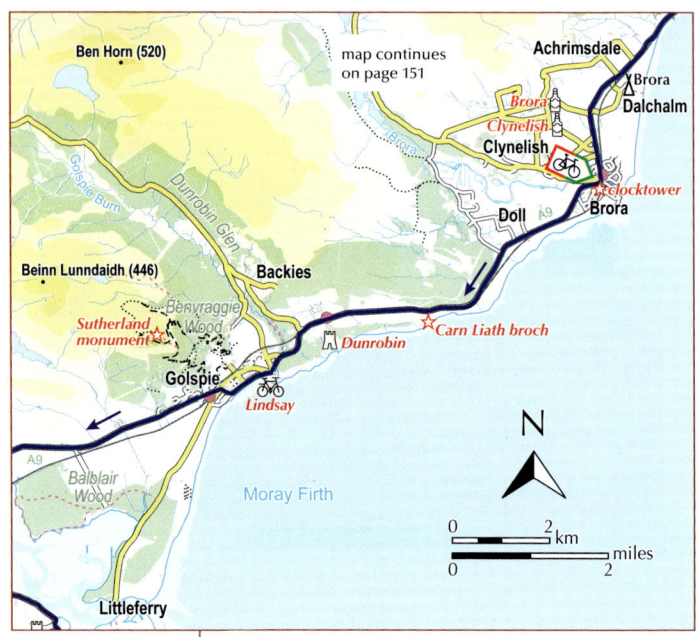

Skelbo castle was built to protect the approach to Little Ferry, the crossing point of Loch Fleet before the Mound causeway was constructed.

Cycle downhill through woods and over Golspie burn, then bear R (Main St) past church R through **Golspie** (6 miles, 4m) (accommodation, refreshments, cycle shop, station). At end of town, pass station L and continue through open country, with flat lands of Loch Fleet estuary L and hills rising R, to reach **The Mound** (9.5 miles, 20m) (accommodation). Cross **Loch Fleet** on 900-metre-long bridge/causeway and continue beside loch L. Where road bears R away from loch, fork L (sp Embo) on narrow country lane winding along lochside and pass ruins of **Skelbo castle** R. ◄ Continue ahead at crossroads and follow road bearing R to pass through **Fourpenny** hamlet. Continue through woods to **Hilton** (accommodation, camping in Embo) and on to reach The Square in centre of **Dornoch** (16.5 miles, 6m) (accommodation, refreshments, camping, cycle shop).

STAGE 14A – BRORA TO TAIN

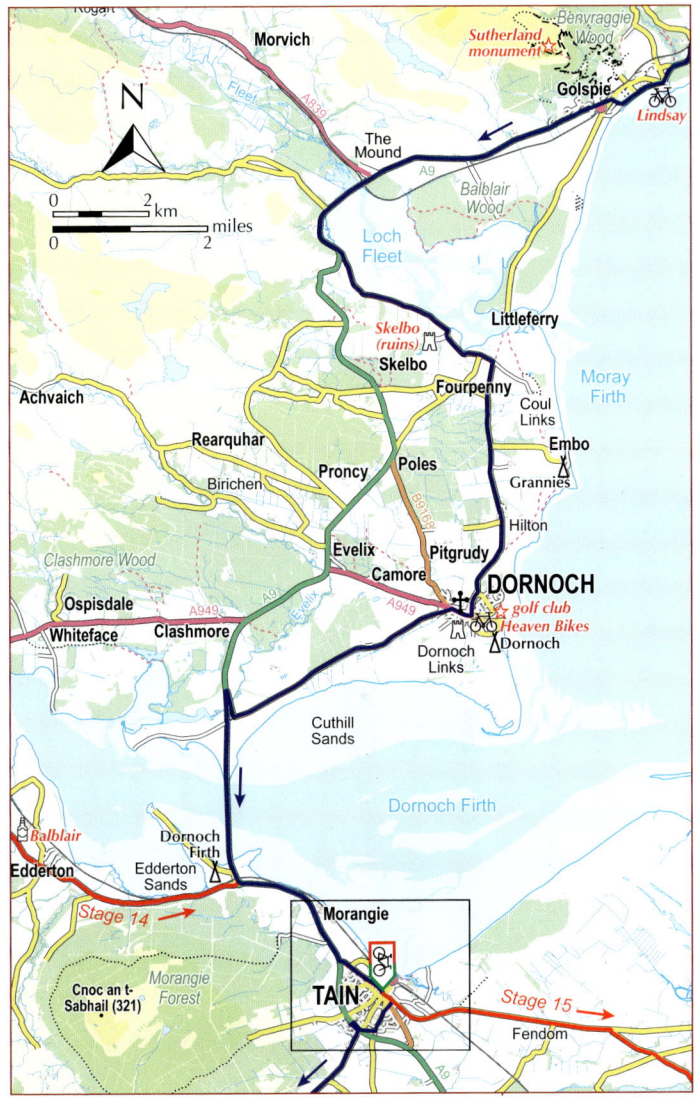

151

DORNOCH

The small but ancient town of Dornoch (pop 1450) is clustered around a 13th-century cathedral and its old bishops' palace (nowadays the Castle hotel). In the churchyard is a medieval stone used by merchants to measure lengths of cloth. A macabre event occurred in 1727 when Janet Horne was tried and found guilty of conspiring with the devil and sentenced to be burnt to death, the last person in Scotland legally executed for witchcraft. East and south of the town, the links of the Royal Dornoch golf club stretch north along the coast and south beside Dornoch Firth. Golf has been played here since the early 17th century, although the present club was not established until 1877. The championship course, the design of which is attributed to Old Tom Morris the professional at St Andrews and four-time winner of the Open championship in the 1860s, is regarded as one of the best in the world.

The cloth-measuring stone in Dornoch cathedral churchyard

Stage 14A – Brora to Tain

Turn R (Castle St) and pass between Castle hotel L and cathedral R. Fork L (Sutherland Rd) in front of old chapel (West church hall) and continue on narrow country lane into open country. Pass Camore wood R and continue past Cuthill house R, then follow road turning R to reach T-junction. Turn L (A9, sp Inverness) and cross bridge over Dornoch Firth estuary, using cycle track L to reach Meikle Ferry roundabout at far end of bridge (22.5 miles, 8m) (refreshments, camping). Turn L at roundabout (A9, first exit, sp Tain) and pass Glenmorangie distillery L.

Fork L (Morangie Rd, B9174, sp Tain industrial estate) and follow road becoming Academy Rd then Tower St to reach tollbooth clocktower L in centre of **Tain** (25 miles, 27m) (accommodation, refreshments, station). ▶

Royal Dornoch golf club has one of the best courses in Scotland

For map and information about Tain see Stage 14

From Tain to North Kessock (opposite Inverness) there is a choice of routes. The main route via the Nigg peninsula and the Black Isle crosses Cromarty Firth by a seasonal ferry which runs from 1 June–30 September, weather conditions permitting. This route is described in Stages 15 and 16. At other times of the year it is necessary to take an alternative route via Dingwall, which is described in Stages 15A and 16A. To check if the ferry is operating: call 07468 417137.

STAGE 15
Tain to Nigg (for Cromarty ferry)

Start	Tain, tollbooth (27m)
Finish	Nigg ferry ramp (5m)
Distance	15 miles (24km)
Ascent	112m
Descent	134m
Waymarking	NCN1

This stage crosses the Nigg peninsula on quiet roads to reach the shore of Cromarty Firth and a seasonal ferry across the firth to Cromarty. It is completely flat over Fendom then gently undulating alongside low hills.

The monument commemorates Kenneth Murray, provost of Tain and local benefactor, who helped fund the restoration of the old collegiate church.

From tollbooth in centre of **Tain**, follow High St (B9174) SE which becomes Lamington St and passes monument erected in 1876 with ornate Gothic arch L. ◄ Where B9174 turns R, continue ahead (Ankerville St, sp Inver). Follow road leaving town then cross railway and continue over flat land known as **Fendom** to reach end of disused runway at Tain airfield (3 miles, 6m).

> **Tain airfield** was operational during World War II, mainly for maritime reconnaissance and escort flights; after the war it became a live firing target range for aircraft from RAF Lossiemouth.

STAGE 15 – TAIN TO NIGG (FOR CROMARTY FERRY)

CYCLING THE NORTH COAST 500

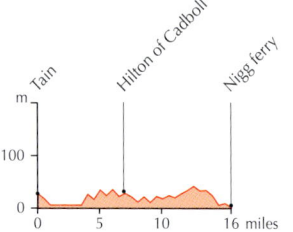

The reproduction Hilton of Cadboll Pictish stone was paid for by Glenmorangie distillery

The Hilton of Cadboll stone is an eighth-century carved Pictish slab now in Edinburgh's Museum of Scotland. The replica at Hilton was commissioned by Glenmorangie, which usees the design on its whisky labels.

Pass turn L for MOD Tain Ranges, then turn next R on easy to miss unmarked road. Go ahead over angled crossroads, passing Newton L. Continue ahead through fields and cross B9165 (sp Hilton) to pass point overlooking site of Pictish stone slab at Hilton of Cadboll L. ◄

Follow road passing above **Hilton of Cadboll** village (7.5 miles, 12m) (accommodation) and continue past **Balintore** (accommodation, refreshments). Road now bears inland away from coast through fields passing Hill of Nigg L (which rises 205m). Turn L (sp Pitcalnie) passing disused church L then continue through **Pitcalnie** (12.5 miles, 36m) and past Nigg Old Church R in **Nigg** village. Where road ahead enters gateway of private drive, turn R. Right turn is unmarked except for black/white direction arrows on opposite side of road. Continue to T-junction

Nigg old church

Stage 15 – Tain to Nigg (for Cromarty ferry)

and turn L (B9175). Pass entrances to Nigg oil terminal and former fabrication yard R and follow road to reach **Nigg ferry** (15 miles, 5m). ▶

> **Nigg fabrication yard** was used to assemble offshore drilling rigs for North Sea oil exploration during the 1970s. It attracted workers from all over Scotland, many of whom made the move permanent with so-called 'Glasgow colonies' establishing themselves in local towns and villages. After rig construction finished, the site was bought by Global Energy Group who use it to repair North Sea installations.

Catch ferry across narrow mouth of Cromarty Firth to **Cromarty** (accommodation, refreshments). Follow red asphalt track away from ferry ramp and continue along Marine Terrace for 200 metres to reach end of stage by harbour R.

> **Cromarty** (pop 650) harbour was more important in the 18th and 19th centuries than it is today, reflected in a number of Georgian merchant houses that together with Victorian fisherman's cottages make up this attractive village. In addition, there is a thatched house in Church Street, birthplace of, and museum commemorating, geologist Hugh Miller. East of the village, Cromarty hall stands on the site of a former castle. There is a pod of bottle-nosed dolphins in the Moray Firth which are often seen close to shore.

Nigg–Cromarty ferry operates daily (1 June to 30 September) every 30 minutes at 15 past and 45 past the hour from 0815–1815.

STAGE 16
Cromarty to Inverness

Start	Cromarty harbour (5m)
Finish	Inverness castle (24m)
Distance	26 miles (42km)
Ascent	416m
Descent	397m
Waymarking	NCN1

After arriving by the short ferry across Cromarty Firth from Nigg, this stage uses waymarked asphalt-surfaced country lanes to traverse the Black Isle peninsula from north to south before leaving on Kessock bridge over Beauly Firth into Inverness. The route climbs over two ridges.

Despite its name, the **Black Isle** (pop 10,250) is neither black nor an island. Rather it is a peninsula bounded by the Cromarty, Moray and Beauly firths known as Black Isle because, as it is generally low-lying, snow lays for fewer days than in neighbouring mountainous areas. Mostly agricultural land, the Black Isle raises cattle and grows barley from which local distilleries produce whisky.

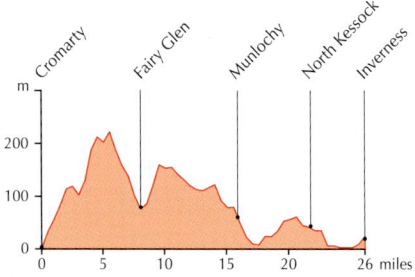

STAGE 16 – CROMARTY TO INVERNESS

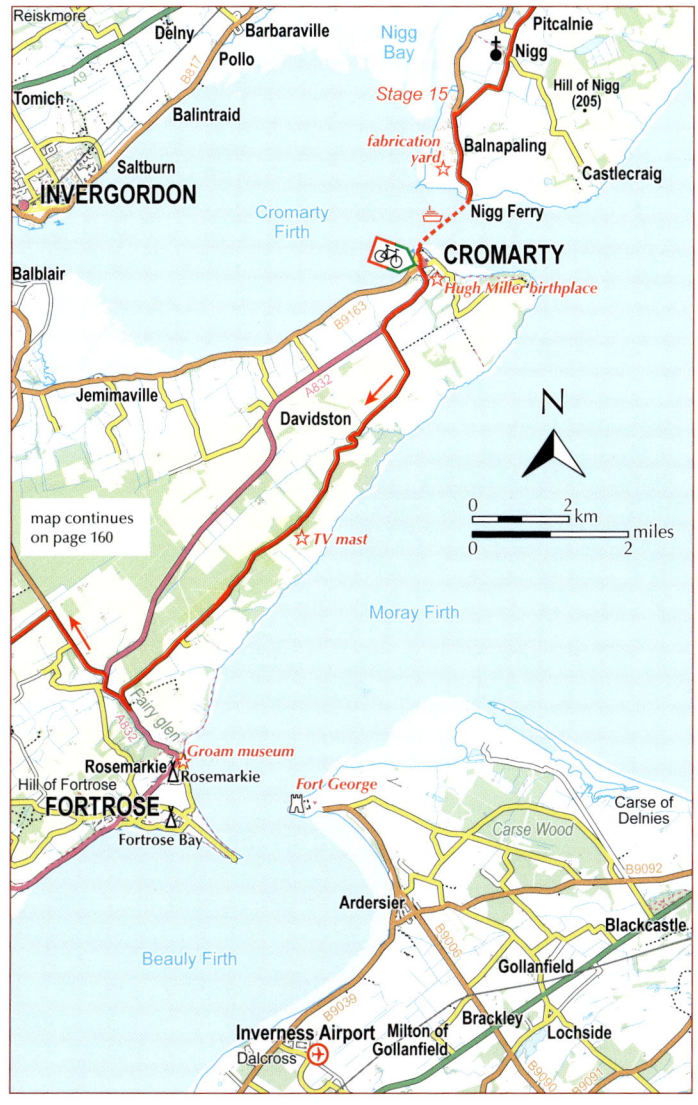

Cycling the North Coast 500

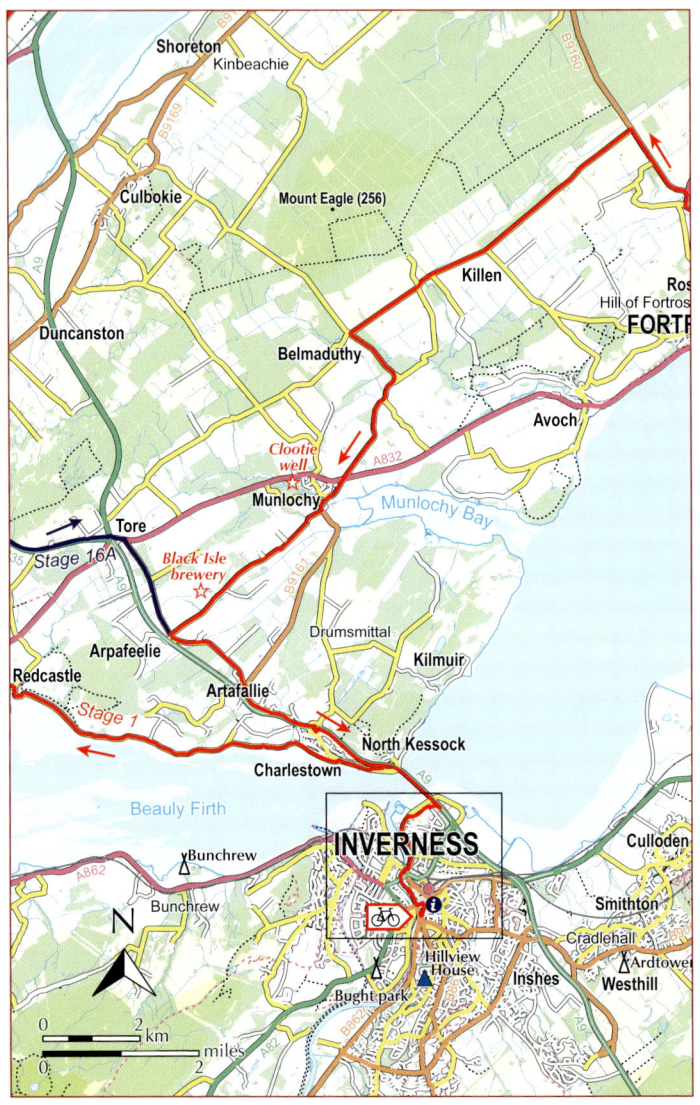

The fertile Black Isle grows barley and raises cattle

From Cromarty harbour, follow Bank St away from quayside and fork first R opposite house 35 into Allan Sq. Bear L (Denoon Pl) then turn R at T-junction and bear immediately L (Denny Rd) beside Victoria Park L. Follow this uphill with ruins of old Gaelic chapel behind trees L and continue out of village into open country. Pass Newton farm R and turn L (sp Eathie), then continue ascending through arable fields. Drop down briefly to cross corrie at head of Eathie burn then continue ascending through woods. Pass **TV transmitter** L to reach summit of Eathie hill (5 miles, 218m).

Descend through woods and fields to T-junction in **Fairy Glen** (8 miles, 80m) and turn sharply R (A832) back through glen. ▶ Pass first turn L and fork L at second (B9160, sp Balblair). Ascend steadily through fields to reach crossroads (161m). Turn L (sp Killen) and continue through **Killen** (12 miles, 122m) to reach T-junction. Turn L through woods and follow road winding downhill to reach staggered crossroads. Dogleg R and L onto Millbank Rd into **Munlochy** (16.5 miles, 14m) (accommodation, refreshments).

Left turn in Fairy Glen leads to Rosemarkie (accommodation, refreshments, camping) a mile away where the Groam House museum, on an ancient monastery site, has a large collection of Pictish religious stones.

Just off the A832, 1km NW of Munlochy, the **Clootie Well** is a forest clearing where trees overhang a sacred spring. In an ancient religious tradition that originated before Christianity came to Scotland, cloots (rags or small pieces of cloth) were soaked in the spring water and used to bathe injured limbs – or even whole people – in the belief that the water had a healing effect. After use the cloots were tied to branches overhanging the spring and left until they rotted away. The assumption was that as they rotted, so the injury or illness would fade away, too. The tradition has lived on and colourful strips of cloth can be seen adorning the clearing.

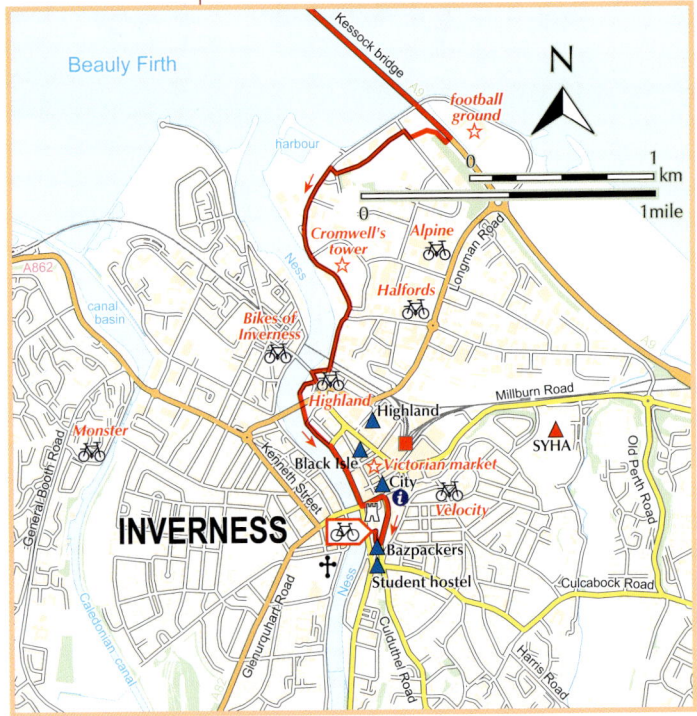

Stage 16 – Cromarty to Inverness

Cycle through village and at end of village turn R opposite church (sp Black Isle brewery). Follow road along valley floor past turn-off R for **Black Isle brewery** at Allangrange Mains then ascend to T-junction at **Arpafeelie** (19 miles, 53m). ▶ Turn L (sp North Kessock) and continue to T-junction at **Artafallie**. Turn R (B9161, sp Inverness) and after 135 metres turn L (sp Coldwell). Cycle downhill through Coldwell into woods and at bottom of descent turn R (sp North Kessock) on short red-asphalt track through trees to reach main road. ▶ Turn L beside layby and continue on cycle track beside A9 main road. After 650 metres, turn sharply L and drop down to pass under main road. Turn L and cross slip road then turn L on cycle track heading back towards A9. Turn R beside main road and continue past **North Kessock** R (accommodation, refreshments) and over Beauly Firth on Kessock bridge. ▶

At end of bridge, turn sharply R and follow asphalt cycle track to reach road. Turn R and first L (Longman Dr) through industrial estate. At end, turn R and L beside Inverness harbour R, then continue into Cromwell Rd. ▶ Continue into Shore St, then go ahead over mini-roundabout and cycle under railway bridge. Turn R through barriers (Portland Pl) then at end, turn L (Waterloo Pl). Turn first R (Riverside St) and just before this reaches car park, fork R to drop down under road bridge. Continue along riverbank (Douglas Row, becoming Bank St) to reach traffic lights beside Ness bridge. Turn L (Bridge St) and where road ahead becomes pedestrian only, follow B861 R (Castle St) gently uphill. ▶ At next traffic lights, in front of Castle Tavern, turn R and immediately R again to reach the end of your journey in front of **Inverness castle** (26 miles, 24m) (accommodation, hostel, refreshments, camping, tourist office, cycle shop, station).

Route via Dingwall (Stages 15A and 16A) rejoins here.

Right turn is easy to miss.

From Kessock bridge the route of Stage 1 is followed in reverse to reach Inverness.

Red sandstone clocktower L (known as Cromwell's tower) stands on the site of a fort ordered to be constructed by Oliver Cromwell.

To go directly to Inverness station, continue ahead along pedestrian street.

STAGE 15A
Tain to Dingwall

Start	Tain, tollbooth (27m)
Finish	Dingwall, High St (10m)
Distance	23 miles (37km)
Ascent	255m
Descent	272m
Waymarking	NCN1 (variant)

This stage uses quiet country roads to contour across the lower slopes of the hills on the north side of Cromarty Firth with only gentle gradients. The route passes through a mixture of forest and agricultural land and the dormitory town of Alness.

See Stage 14 for a map of Tain.

The monument commemorates Kenneth Murray, provost of Tain and local benefactor who helped fund the restoration of the old collegiate church.

◀ From tollbooth in centre of **Tain**, follow High St (B9174) SE and continue into Lamington St passing monument erected in 1879 with ornate Gothic arch L. ◀ Follow B9174 turning R (Geanies St) beside house 31. Continue ahead over crossroads into Hartfield St and bear L (Hartfield Rd) passing Tain Royal academy R. Turn R at crossroads (Cameron Rd) then pass modern church L and continue into Vincent St. Turn L opposite house 18 onto underpass beneath A9 Tain bypass then turn sharply L on cycle track parallel with main road. At end turn R

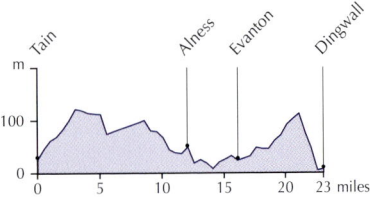

STAGE 15A – TAIN TO DINGWALL

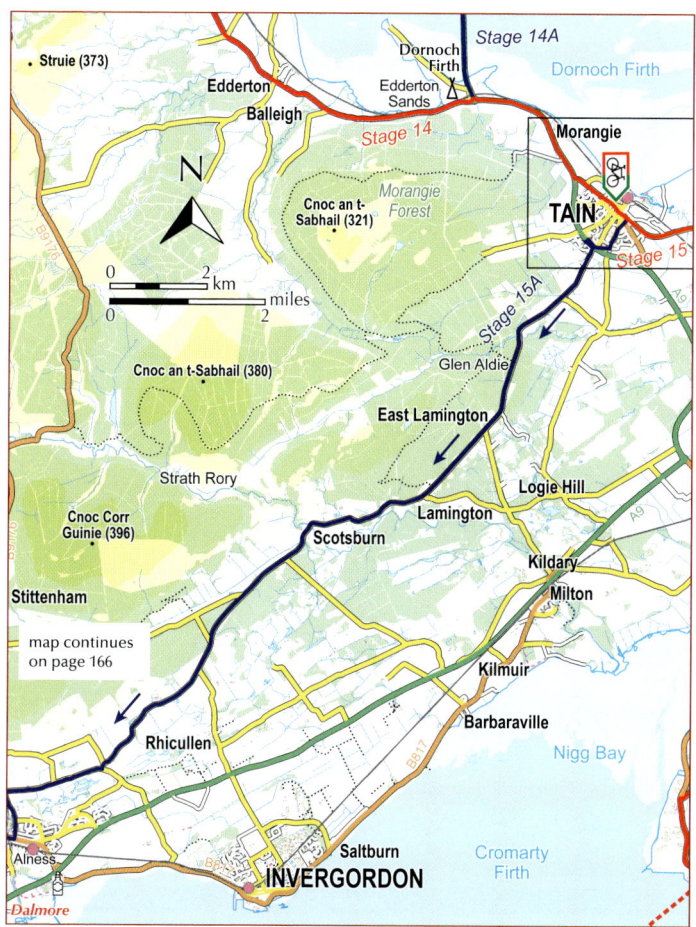

(Scotsburn Rd) and continue gently uphill through **Glen Aldie** into forest to reach summit (116m). Cycle ahead through **Lamington** (4 miles, 111m) and **Scotsburn** then cross bridge over river Balnagowan. Continue through forest and fields then descend gently to T-junction at Balnaguisich (10.5 miles, 46m). Turn R (sp Alness) then

CYCLING THE NORTH COAST 500

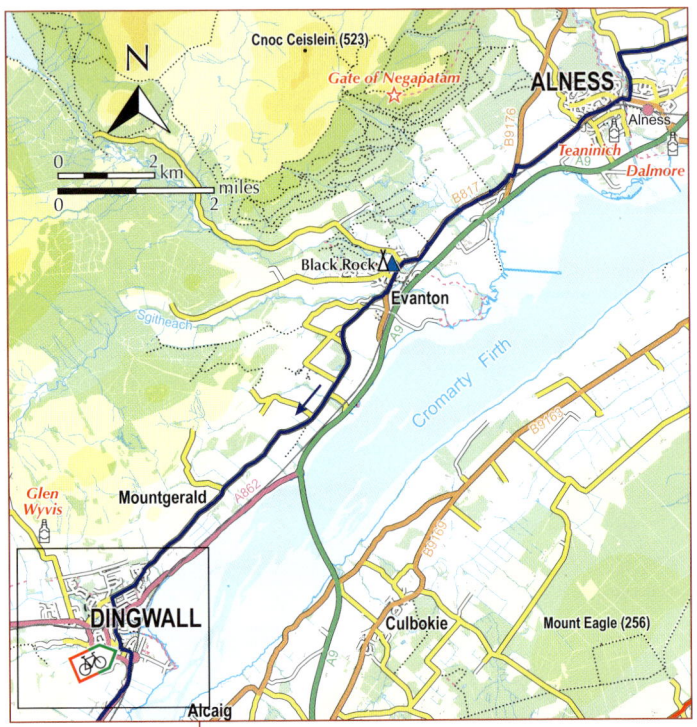

continue to next T-junction and turn L (sp Alness). Follow road past golf club R and continue on Ardross St to T-junction in centre of **Alness** (12.5 miles, 24m) (accommodation, refreshments, station).

ALNESS

Alness (pop 6000) is known for its floral displays and has won the Britain in Bloom award five times in the last 25 years. Although it no longer enters the competition on the grounds of cost, local volunteers still produce attractive displays every summer. There are two distilleries in the town: Dalmore, which produces award-winning single malts, and Teaninich, which produces

STAGE 15A – TAIN TO DINGWALL

whisky for blending, much of which goes for use in Johnnie Walker Red Label. The flats below the town beside the Cromarty Firth were the site of a World War II air station for Catalina and Sunderland flying boats operating off the coast of Scotland. A Catalina propeller has been preserved in the town. On top of Cnoc Fyrish, 3 miles west of Alness, a large monument representing the Gate of Negapatam in southeast India can be seen from most points in town. Negapatam was captured for the British in 1781 by General Munro, a local landowner who served in India. The monument was constructed during the clearances as a work-creation project for crofters evicted from their farms.

Turn R (High St, B817, sp Evanton) then cross bridge over river Averon and continue ahead on Novar Rd. Just after bus stop R, fork R on cycle track following route of old road. Cross side road and bridge over stream then follow track back to main road beside cemetery. Continue beside road, using cycle track R, to reach T-junction. ▶ Turn L (sp Evanton), then after 300 metres turn R (B817, sp Evanton) and continue on cycle track initially beside road R but soon bearing R on gravel track

The Gate of Negapatam monument is visible on the hilltop to the right.

Alness has won the Britain in Bloom award five times in 25 years

through forest edge. This cycle track is continuous as far as Evanton although it does cross and re-cross road several times. Where cycle track ends soon after beginning of Evanton, follow road ahead over river Glass to reach centre of **Evanton** (16.5 miles, 28m) (accommodation, hostel, refreshments, camping).

> **Evanton** (pop 1400) stands on a spit of land between the rivers Glass (which flows through attractive Black Rock gorge just north of Evanton) and Sgitheach. It was built in the 19th century as a planned resettlement village by Alexander Fraser of Balconie to house crofters evicted during clearance of his local estates. He named it after his son Evan. Nowadays it is a commuter village with most of the residents commuting to work in nearby towns such as Dingwall, Invergordon and Inverness.

Pass through town on Balconie St then cross river Sgitheach and turn R beside war memorial (Drummond Rd). Continue into open country through fields past series of farms, climbing gently to summit at **Mountgerald** (20.5 miles, 112m) (refreshments) then descend into Dingwall on Old Evanton Rd. Just after house 1 on R, turn L (Tulloch Ave, sp Town centre) downhill through housing estate to traffic lights. Turn R (A862) then fork L (Craig Rd, sp Town centre) passing over railway crossing. Continue into Tulloch St to reach stage end at T-junction with High St in centre of **Dingwall** (23 miles, 10m) (accommodation, refreshments, camping, cycle shop, station).

DINGWALL

Dingwall (pop 5400) gets its name from Ping Vǒllr, Norse for meeting field, a root it shares with ancient parliaments, Tynwald in the Isle of Man and Pingvellir in Iceland. The original field now lies beneath a car park beside an obelisk commemorating the First Earl of Cromartie. There are plans to create a visitor centre on the site. The Vikings built a fort on the shore of Cromarty Firth, which developed in medieval times into one of the largest castles in

STAGE 15A – TAIN TO DINGWALL

northern Scotland. This was abandoned in 1625 and subsequently used as a stone quarry for construction work in Dingwall. The site has been levelled and very little remains. An escape tunnel ran for 800 metres to Tulloch castle north of Dingwall but, as this has partly collapsed, it cannot be visited. In recent years Dingwall has become known throughout Scotland for the rise of Ross County, the local football team that progressed from local amateur football in 1994 to the Scottish premier league in 2012, a level they maintained against all odds, even winning their first major trophy, the Scottish League cup in 2016. Their average attendance in the premier league of over 4000 is only just short of the town's population, making County the best per capita supported team in Britain.

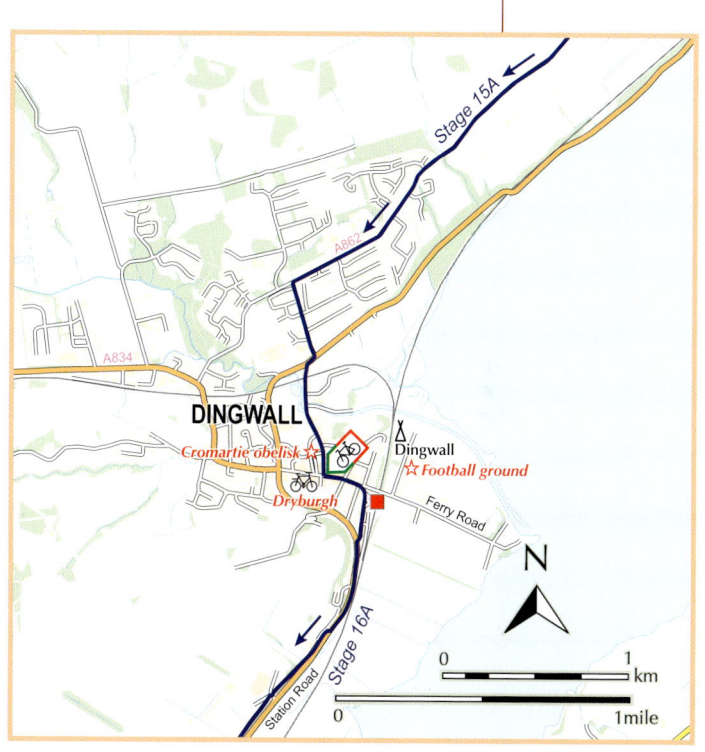

STAGE 16A

Dingwall to Inverness

Start	Dingwall, High St (10m)
Finish	Inverness castle (24m)
Distance	14.5 miles (23.5km)
Ascent	201m
Descent	187m
Waymarking	NCN1 (variant)

This short final stage follows cycle tracks beside main roads across a corner of the Black Isle, then crosses Kessock bridge to finish in Inverness. There is a steady climb from the Cromarty Firth to 149m, then an equally steady descent to Beauly Firth.

From junction with Tulloch St in **Dingwall**, follow High St E. Continue into Station Rd, bearing R past station and follow this to traffic lights. Turn L (Greenhill St, sp Inverness) and continue out of town. At beginning of Pitglassie, fork R onto cycle track along route of old road parallel with main road and follow this to reach roundabout at edge of **Maryburgh** (refreshments). Turn L across road before roundabout and follow cycle track L beside A835 (sp Inverness) across bridges over railway and river Conon onto the **Black Isle**.

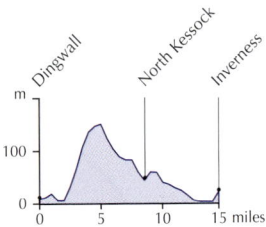

STAGE 16A – DINGWALL TO INVERNESS

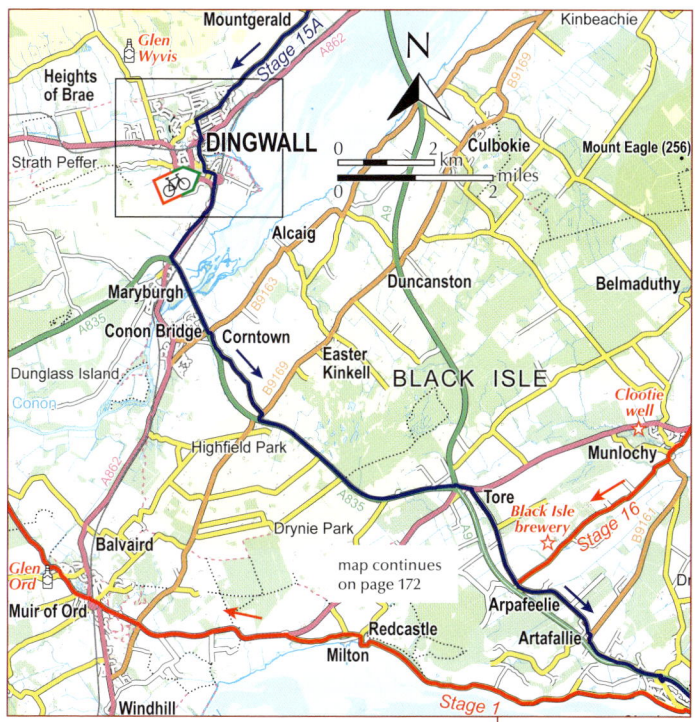

Ascend beside main road, then turn L (B9163, sp Alcaig) and immediately R (sp Torgorm) on country road. Follow this ascending through fields to second crossroads and turn R beside small cottage. After 100 metres, turn L (A835, sp Inverness) on cycle track L of road and follow this ascending through Newton (accommodation) to reach summit (149m). Continue downhill across turn-off to Muckernich then pass large digital traffic sign and fork L uphill away from main road to roundabout in **Tore** (6.5 miles, 84m).

Go ahead across A9 then fork L beside next exit (A832, sp Fortrose). After 250 metres, turn R beside white and red house onto country road between woods

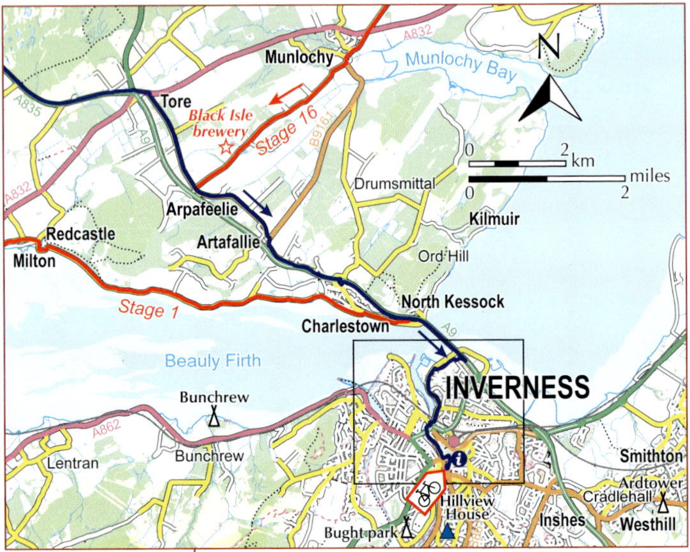

CYCLING THE NORTH COAST 500

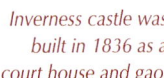

and fields. Continue past **Arpafeelie** junction (8 miles, 53m), where Stage 16 via Cromarty is joined, to reach T-junction at **Artafallie**. Turn R (B9161, sp Inverness) and follow route description in Stage 16 continuing past **North Kessock** (accommodation, refreshments) and over Kessock bridge to reach stage end at **Inverness castle** (14.5 miles, 24m) (accommodation, hostel, refreshments, camping, tourist office, cycle shop, station). ◀

For map of Inverness see Stage 16

Inverness castle was built in 1836 as a court house and gaol

APPENDIX A
Facilities summary

	Distance (miles)	Cum. distance (miles)	Altitude (m)	Accommodation	Hostel	Meals	Camping	Tourist office	Cycle shop	Station
Stage 1										
Inverness	0	0	24	x	x	x	x	x	x	x
North Kessock	3.5	3.5	4	x		x				
Muir of Ord	8.5	12	35	x		x	x		x	x
Marybank	4	16	25	x						
Contin	2.5	18.5	29	x		x	x		x	
Garve	6	24.5	72							x
Stage 2										
Lochluichart	5	29.5	102	x						x
Achanalt	4.5	34	125							x
Achnasheen	6.5	40.5	155	x	x	x				x
Craig	10	50.5	78		x					
Achnashellach	2.5	53	42							x
Strathcarron (off-route)	5.5	58.5	7	x		x				x
Lochcarron	2.5	61	5	x		x	x			
Stage 3										
Ardarroch	5	66	31		x	x				
Tornapress	2	68	3			x				
Shieldaig	8.5	76.5	4	x		x	x			

Cycling the North Coast 500

	Distance (miles)	Cum. distance (miles)	Altitude (m)	Accommodation	Hostel	Meals	Camping	Tourist office	Cycle shop	Station
Stage 3A										
Ardarroch	5	(5)	31		x	x				
Tornapress	2	(7)	3			x				
Applecross	11	(18)	5	x	x	x	x			
Callakille	8	(26)	28	x						
Shieldaig	16.5	(42.5)	4	x		x	x			
Stage 4										
Annat	6	82.5	5	x		x				
Torridon	1.5	84	12	x	x	x	x			
Kinlochewe	9.5	93.5	32	x	x	x	x			
Taagan	1.5	95	23				x			
Talladale	8	103	14	x		x				
Charlestown	9	112	5	x		x				
Gairloch	1	113	12	x	x	x	x	x		
Stage 5										
Poolewe	5.5	118.5	9	x		x	x			
Drumchork	6	124.5	17	x						
Aultbea	0.5	125	24	x		x				
Laide	2	127	29	x			x			
Badcaul	10.5	137.5	78				x			
Camusnagaul	3.5	141	16	x						
Dundonnel	2	143	4	x		x				
Lael	15.5	158.5	42		x					
Ardcharnich	5	163.5	28	x						

Appendix A – Facilities summary

	Distance (miles)	Cum. distance (miles)	Altitude (m)	Accommodation	Hostel	Meals	Camping	Tourist office	Cycle shop	Station
Braes of Ullapool	4	167.5	38	x						
Ullapool	0.5	168	9	x	x	x	x	x		
Stage 6										
Morefield	0.5	168.5	24	x						
Ardmair	3	171.5	5	x			x			
Strathcanaird	3.5	175	80	x						
Elphin	7.5	182.5	145		x					
Altnacaelgach (off-route)	3	185.5	148	x		x				
Inchnadamph	6	191.5	73	x	x	x				
Lochinver	12	203.5	4	x	x	x				
Stage 7										
Achmelvich beach (off-route)	2	205.5	7		x	x	x			
Clachtoll	3.5	209	13				x			
Stoer	1	210	46	x						
Drumbeg	7	217	45	x		x				
Unapool	10	227	40	x		x				
Kylesku (off-route)	1	228	25	x		x				
Stage 8										
Lower Badcall	7.5	235.5	25	x		x				
Scourie	2.5	238	18	x		x	x		x	
Rhiconich	11	249	15	x		x				
Durness	14	263	40	x	x	x	x			

CYCLING THE NORTH COAST 500

	Distance (miles)	Cum. distance (miles)	Altitude (m)	Accommodation	Hostel	Meals	Camping	Tourist office	Cycle shop	Station
Stage 9										
Lerinmore	1	264	32	x	x	x				
Laid	7	271	40	x						
Tongue	21.5	292.5	45	x	x	x	x			
Stage 10										
Strath Tongue	3.5	296	70	x						
Borgie (off-route)	3.5	299.5	32	x			x			
Invernaver	4.5	304	19	x						
Bettyhill	1.5	305.5	60	x		x	x			
Armadale	6	311.5	23	x						
Strathy	3.5	315	5	x			x			
Melvich	3.5	318.5	56	x		x	x			
Halladale	1.5	320	8							
Stage 11										
Forss	10	330	17	x			x			
Burnside	5	335	22	x			x			
Thurso	0.5	335.5	10	x	x	x	x		x	x
Murkle	3.5	339	31	x			x			
Castletown	1.5	340.5	23	x			x			
Dunnet	3.5	344	20	x		x	x			
Mey	4.5	348.5	37	x			x			
East Mey	1.5	350	63	x	x					
Gills	1	351	35	x			x			
John o' Groats	4.5	355.5	5	x		x	x	x		

Appendix A – Facilities summary

	Distance (miles)	Cum. distance (miles)	Altitude (m)	Accommodation	Hostel	Meals	Camping	Tourist office	Cycle shop	Station
Stage 12										
Upper Gills	4	359.5	54	x						
Castletown	10.5	370	23	x		x				
Thurso	6	376	10	x	x	x	x		x	x
Melvich (off-route)	16	392	8	x		x	x			
Stage 13										
Achiemore	4	396	30		x					
Forsinard	10	406	154	x						x
Kinbrace	7	413	129							x
Garvault hotel	8	421	165	x		x				
Altnaharra	19.5	440.5	82	x		x				
Stage 14										
Crask Inn	7.5	448	230	x		x				
Dalchork	10	458	102				x			
Lairg	3	461	85	x		x				x
Falls of Shin	4.5	465.5	45			x				
Invershin	3	468.5	10	x	x	x				x
Culrain	0.5	469	22							x
Ardgay	4	473	4	x		x			x	x
Edderton	8.5	481.5	23	x						x
Meikle Ferry	3	484.5	9			x	x			
Tain	2.5	487	27	x		x				x
Stage 12A										
Auckengill	6	361.5	33	x						

CYCLING THE NORTH COAST 500

	Distance (miles)	Cum. distance (miles)	Altitude (m)	Accommodation	Hostel	Meals	Camping	Tourist office	Cycle shop	Station
Keiss	2	363.5	28	x		x				
Wick	8.5	372	8	x		x	x		x	x
Thrumster	4	376	74	x		x				
Occumster	8	384	73	x						
Lybster	1.5	385.5	68	x		x				
Stage 13A										
Forse	2	387.5	76	x						
Latheronwheel	2.5	390	64	x						
Laidhay	2	392	73			x				
Dunbeath	1	393	25	x		x	x			
Berriedale	5.5	398.5	10			x				
Navidale	8	406.5	54	x						
Helmsdale	1	407.5	10	x	x	x				x
Portgower	1.5	409	45	x						
Dalchalm	8.5	417.5	13				x			
Brora	1	418.5	11	x		x				x
Stage 14A										
Dunrobin castle	4.5	423	55			x				x
Golspie	1.5	424.5	4	x		x			x	x
The Mound	3.5	428	36	x						
Hilton	5.5	433.5	36	x			x			
Dornoch	1.5	435	6	x		x	x		x	
Meikle Ferry	6	441	8			x	x			
Tain	2.5	443.5	27	x		x				x

Appendix A – Facilities summary

	Distance (miles)	Cum. distance (miles)	Altitude (m)	Accommodation	Hostel	Meals	Camping	Tourist office	Cycle shop	Station
Stage 15										
Hilton of Cadboll	7.5	494.5	12	x						
Balintore	1.5	496	15	x		x				
Cromarty	6	502	5	x		x				
Stage 16										
Rosemarkie (off-route)	9	(511)	15	x		x	x			
Munlochy	8.5	518.5	14	x		x				
North Kessock	6	524.5	27	x		x				
Inverness	3.5	528	24	x	x	x	x	x	x	x
Stage 15A										
Alness	12.5	499.5	24	x		x				x
Evanton	4	503.5	28	x	x	x	x			
Mountgerald	4	507.5	112			x				
Dingwall	2.5	510	10	x		x	x		x	x
Stage 16A										
Maryburgh	1.5	511.5	12			x				
Newton	3	514.5	146	x						
North Kessock	7	521.5	27	x		x				
Inverness	3	524.5	24	x	x	x	x	x	x	x

APPENDIX B
Tourist information

Tourist offices

Inverness (VisitScotland iCentre)
36 High St
IV1 1JQ
01463 252401
www.visitscotland.com

Gairloch (The Gale Centre)
Achtercairn
IV21 2BH
01445 712071
www.galeactionforum.co.uk

Ullapool (VisitScotland iCentre)
Argyle St
IV26 2UB
01854 612486
www.visitscotland.com

John o' Groats (commercial tourist office)
KW1 4YR
01955 611373
www.visitjohnogroats.com

Online information

Scottish national tourist organisation
www.visitscotland.com

Lochcarron
www.lochcarron.org.uk

Applecross
www.applecross.uk.com

Torridon and Shieldaig
www.stevecarter.com/sh.htm

Gairloch and Poolewe
www.visitwester-ross.com

Ullapool
www.ullapool.com

Scourie
www.scourie.co.uk

Durness
www.visitdurness.com

Thurso
www.discoverthurso.co.uk

Caithness and Sutherland
www.venture-north.co.uk

Lairg
wwwlairgandrogart.co.uk

Helmsdale
www.helmsdale.scot

Brora
www.broravillage.scot

Dornoch
www.visitdornoch.com

The Black Isle
www.black-isle.info

APPENDIX C
Hostels and bunkhouses

Inverness

SYHA (155 beds)
Victoria Dr
Inverness
IV2 3QB
01463 231771
www.hostellingscotland.org.uk

Bazpackers hostel (34 beds)
4 Culduthel Rd
Inverness
IV2 4AB
01463 717663
www.bazpackershostel.co.uk

Highland Backpackers hostel (24 beds)
24 Rose St
Inverness
IV1 1NQ
01463 241962
www.highland-backpackers-hostel

Inverness Student hostel (57 beds)
8 Culduthel Rd
Inverness
IV2 4AB
01463 236556
www.invernessstudenthotel.com

City hostel (basic) (79 beds)
23a High St
Inverness
IV1 1HY
01463 221225
cityhostelinverness@yahoo.com

Hillview House hostel (16 beds)
Merlewood Rd
Inverness
IV2 4NL
07581 111200
www.invernesshostel.co.uk

Black Isle hostel (54 beds plus 14 single rooms)
47–49 Academy St
Inverness
IV1 1LP
01463 233933
www.blackislebrewery.com/hostel

Stage 2

Ledgowan Lodge bunkhouse (5 beds)
A890
Achnasheen
IV22 2EJ
01445 720252
www.ledgowanlodge.co.uk

Gerry's hostel (20 beds)
A890
Craig
IV54 8YU
01520 766232
https://gerryshostel.com

Stage 3

Sanachan bunkhouse (15 beds)
Kishorn
IV54 8XA
01520 733484
www.ourscottishadventure.com

Hartfield House hostel (48 beds)
(SYHA affiliated)
Applecross
IV54 8ND
01520 733484
www.hartfieldhouse.org.uk

Stage 4
SYHA (51 beds)
Torridon
IV22 2EZ
01445 791284
www.hostellingscotland.org.uk

Kinlochewe bunkhouse (12 beds)
Kinlochewe
IV22 2PA
01445 760253
www.kinlochewehotel.co.uk

Gairloch Sands SYHA (31 beds)
Carn Dearg (2.5 miles off-route)
Gairloch
IV21 2DJ
01445 712219
www.hostellingscotland.org.uk

Stage 5
Forest Way bunkhouse (11 beds)
4 Lael
IV23 2RS
07912 177419
www.forestway.co.uk

SYHA (44 beds)
22 Shore St
Ullapool
IV26 2UJ
01854 612254
www.hostellingscotland.org.uk

The Ceilidh Place bunkhouse (32 beds)
14 West Argyle St
Ullapool
IV26 2TY
01854 612103
www.theceilidhplace.com

Stage 6
Inchnadamph Lodge hostel (32 beds)
Inchnadamph
IV27 4HL
01571 822218
www.inchnadamph.com

An Cala Café bunkhouse (14 beds)
Culag Park
Lochinver
IV27 4LE
01571 844598
www.ancalacafeandbunkhouse.co.uk

Stage 7
Achmelvich Beach SYHA (20 beds)
(2 miles off-route)
Rhicarn
IV27 4JB
01571 844480
www.hostellingscotland.org.uk

Stoer hostel (22 beds)
B869
Stoer
IV27 4JE
01571 855388
www.stoerhostel.co.uk

Stage 8
Lazy Crofter bunkhouse (20 beds)
Durness
IV27 4PN
01971 511202
www.visitdurness.com

APPENDIX C – HOSTELS AND BUNKHOUSES

Stage 9
SYHA (31 beds)
Smoo
Leirinmore
IV27 4QA
01971 511264
www.hostellingscotland.org.uk

Kyle of Tongue hostel (20 beds)
Tongue
IV27 4XH
01847 611789
www.tonguehostelandholidaypark.co.uk

Stage 11
Sandra's Backpackers hostel (26 beds)
24 Princes St
Thurso
KW14 7BQ
01847 894575
www.sandras-backpackers.co.uk

Highland Haven (10 beds)
St Johns
East Mey
KW14 8XL
07377 267555
www.thehighlandhaven.co.uk

Stage 13
Corn Mill bunkhouse (14 beds)
Achiemore
Strathhalladale
KW13 6YT
01641 571219
www.cornmillbunkhouse.co.uk

Stage 14
Invershin Hotel bunkhouse (10 beds)
Invershin
IV27 4ET
01549 421202
www.invershin.com

Stage 13A
Helmsdale hostel (22 beds)
(SYHA affiliated)
Stafford St
Helmsdale
KW8 6JR
07971 922356
www.helmsdalehostel.co.uk

Stage 15A
Black Rock bunkhouse (16 beds)
28 Balconie St (B817)
Evanton
IV16 9UN
01349 830917
www.blackrockscotland.com

APPENDIX D
Campsites

Stage 1
Bught Park
Bught Lane
Inverness
IV3 5SR
01463 236920
www.invernesscaravanpark.com

Ardtower caravan park (3 miles off-route, uphill)
Culloden Rd
Cradlehall
Inverness
IV2 5AA
01463 790555
www.ardtower-caravanpark.com

Bunchrew caravan park (3.5 miles off-route)
Bunchrew A862
Inverness
IV3 8TD
01463 237802
www.bunchrew-caravanpark.co.uk

Beauly holiday park (4 miles from Muir of Ord)
Lovat bridge A862
Beauly
IV4 7AY
www.beaulyholidaypark.scot

Riverside caravan park and campsite
Contin
IV14 9ES
01463 513599
www.lochness-chalets.co.uk

Stage 2
Ledgowan Lodge campsite
Achnasheen
IV22 2EJ
01445 720252
www.ledgowanlodge.co.uk

The Wee campsite
Croft Rd
Lochcarron
IV54 8YA
07876 642355

Stage 3A
Applecross campsite
Mains of Applecross
IV54 8ND
01520 744268
https://visitapplecross.com

Stage 3/3A
Shieldaig (camping and cabins)
Aurora, Temperance Brae
Shieldaig
01520 755224
IV54 8XN
www.shieldaigcampingandcabins.co.uk

Stage 4
Torridon NTS free campsite
Just off A896
IV22 2EZ
01445 712345

Kinlochewe caravan club site
A832
IV22 2PA
01445 760239
www.caravanclub.co.uk

Beinn Eighe NTS free campsite
Taagen
1.5 miles from Kinlochewe
A832
IV22 2PD

Gairloch caravan park
I Mihol Rd
Strath
IV21 2BX
01445 712373
www.gairlochholidaypark.co.uk

Sands caravan and camping
(3.5 miles from Gairloch)
Big Sand
Gairloch
IV21 2DL
01445 712152
www.sandscaravanandcamping.co.uk

Stage 5
Inverewe Gardens campsite
Poolewe
IV22 2LF
01445 781249
www.campingandcaravanclub.co.uk

Gruinard bay caravan park
Laide
01445 731556
IV22 2ND
www.gruinardbay.co.uk

Northern Lights camping and caravan park
1 Cnoc Dubh
Badcaul
IV23 2QY
01697 371379

Stage 6
Broomfield holiday park
West Lane
Ullapool
IV26 2UT
01854 612020
www.broomfieldhp.com

Ardmair Point holiday park
Ardmair
A835
IV26 2TN
01854 612054
www.ardmair.com

Stage 7
Shore caravan site (2 miles off-route)
106 Achmelvich Beach
Lochinver
IV27 4JB
01571 844393
www.shorecaravansite.co.uk

Clachtoll Beach campsite
134 Clachtoll
IV27 4JD
01571 855377
www.clachtollbeachcampsite.com

Stage 8
Scourie caravan and camping
A894
Scourie
IV27 4TE
07496 366933
www.scouriecampsitesutherland.com

Sango Sands Oasis
Durness
IV27 4PZ
01971 511726
www.sangosands.com

Bayview campsite
(3 miles off-route)
Talmine
IV27 4YS
07849 609339
www.bayviewcampsite.co.uk

Stage 9

Kyle of Tongue hostel campsite
Tongue
IV27 4XH
01847 611789
www.tonguehostelandholidaypark.co.uk

Stage 10

Craigdhu caravan and camping site
Dunveaden House
Bettyhill
KW14 7SP
01641 521273

North Coast touring park
Halladale Inn
Melvich
KW14 7YJ
01641 531282
www.thehalladaleinn.co.uk

Stage 11

Thurso Bay caravan and camping park
Smith Terrace
Thurso
KW14 7JY
01847 892244
www.thursobaycamping.co.uk

Dunnet Bay caravan club site
Dunnet
KW14 8XD
01847 821319
www.caravanclub.co.uk

Windhaven camping
(2 miles off-route)
Brough
KW14 8YE
07590 428183
www.windhaven.co.uk

Ferry View camping
Gauze cottage
Gills
KW1 4YB
07591 540400
www.ferryview.scot

John o' Groats caravan and camping site
County Rd
John o' Groats
KW1 4YR
01955 611329
www.johnogroatscampsite.co.uk

Stage 14

Pondside camping
(1 mile off-route)
4 Tirryside
Lairg
IV27 4DL
07902 947331
www.pondside.co.uk

Woodend camping and caravan park
(2.5 miles off-route)
Achnairn
IV27 4DN
01549 402248

Dornoch Firth caravan park
Meikle Ferry South
IV19 1JX
01862 892292
www.dornochfirth.co.uk

APPENDIX D – CAMPSITES

Stage 12A
Wick caravan and camping site
Riverside Drive
Wick
KW1 5SP
07563 388826
www.wickcampsite.co.uk

Stage 13A
Inver caravan park
Houstry Rd
Dunbeath
KW6 6EH
01593 731441
www.inver-caravan-park.co.uk

Brora caravan club site
Saltire
Dalchalm
KW9 6LP
01408 621479
www.caravanclub.co.uk

Stage 14A
Grannie's Heilan' Hame holiday park
Embo
IV25 3QD
0344 335 2271
www.parkdeanresorts.co.uk

Dornoch caravan and camp park
The Links
Dornoch
IV25 3LX
01862 810423
www.dornochcaravans.co.uk

Stage 16
Rosemarkie camping and caravanning club site (1.5 miles off-route)
Ness Rd East
Rosemarkie
IV10 8SE
01381 621117
www.campingandcaravanningclub.co.uk

Fortrose Bay campsite (2 miles off-route)
Wester Greengates
Fortrose
IV10 8RX
01381 621927
www.fortrosebaycampsite.co.uk

Stage 15A
Black Rock caravan and camping park
28 Balconie St (B817)
Evanton
IV16 9UN
01349 830917
www.blackrockscotland.com

Dingwall camping and caravanning club site
Jubilee Park Rd
Dingwall
IV15 9QZ
01349 862236
www.campingandcaravanningclub.co.uk

APPENDIX E
Cycle shops and cycle hire

Cycle shops

Inverness
Alpine Bikes
2 Henderson Rd
Inverness
IV1 1SN
01463 729171
www.tiso.com

Bikes of Inverness
39 Grant St
Inverness
IV3 6BP
01463 225965
www.bikesofinverness.co.uk

Halfords
Harbour Rd
Inverness
IV1 1SY
01463 223388
www.halfords.com

Highland Bikes
29 Shore St
Inverness
IV1 1NG
01463 234789
www.highlandbikes.com

Monsterbike
9 Canal Rd
Inverness
IV3 8NF
01463 729500
www.monsterbikeshop.com

Velocity café & bicycle workshop
1 Crown Ave
Inverness
IV2 3NF
01463 419956
www.velocitylove.co.uk

Stage 1
Orange Fox
2 Industrial estate
Gt North Rd
Muir of Ord
IV6 7UA
01463 870346
07775 690076 24hr mobile repair service
www.orangefoxbikes.co.uk

Square Wheels
The Square
Strathpeffer
(off-route, 3 miles from Contin)
IV14 9DW
01997 421000
07538 011622 for emergency out of hours enquiries
www.squarewheels.biz

Stage 8
Barnes, Bits and Bikes (repairs only)
Gardener's Cottage
Scourie
IV27 4SX
01971 502259
www.spanglefish.com/barnesbitsandbikes

Appendix E – Cycle shops and cycle hire

Stage 11
The Bike Shop
35 High St
Thurso
KW14 8AZ
01847 895385
facebook.com/thebikeshopthurso

Stage 12A
The Spot
Francis St
Wick
KW1 5PZ
01955 602698

Stage 14
Heaven Bikes
Lairg Rd
Bonar Bridge
off-route, 1 mile from Ardgay
IV24 3EA
01863 766219 or 07543 466699
www.heavenbikes.co.uk

Stage 14A
Lindsay and Co
Main St
Golspie
KW10 6RA
01408 633212 (07787 161653 for limited out-of-hours service)

Heaven Bikes
The Hub
1 Argyll St
Dornoch
IV25 3LA
07543 466699
www.heavenbikes.co.uk

Stage 15A
Dryburgh Cycles
9 Tulloch St
Dingwall
IV15 9JY
01349 862163
www.dryburghcycles.com

Cycle hire
Ticket to Ride
The Pavilion, Bellfield Park
Inverness
IV2 4SZ
01463 419160
www.tickettoridehighlands.co.uk

APPENDIX F
Munros near route (mountains over 914m)

	height	start	summit
Stage 1			
Ben Wyvis	1046m	NH410671	NH463684
Stage 2			
Moruisg	926m	NH080520	NH101500
Sgùrr a Chaorachain	1053m	NH039493	NH088447
Sgùrr Chionnich	979m	NH039493	NH076446
Beinn Liath Mhor	926m	NH004483	NG964520
Sgùrr Ruadh	962m	NG959505	NH004483
Maol Chean-dearg	933m	NG956451	NG924499
Stage 4			
Mullach an Rathain	1023m	NG914554	NG912577
Spidean a'Choire Leith (Liathach)	1055m	NG935566	NG929580
Ruadh-stac Mor (Beinn Eighe)	1010m	NG958569	NG951612
Spidean Coire nan Clach (Beinn Eighe)	993m	NG966598	NG977578
Slioch	981m	NH038624	NH005691
Stage 5			
Bidein a'Ghlas Thuill (An Teallach)	1062m	NH093878	NH069844
Sgurr Fiona (An Teallach)	1060m	NH093878	NH064837
A'Chailleach	997m	NH163761	NH136714
Sgùrr Breac	999m	NH163761	NH158711
Meall a'Chrasgaidh	934m	NH163761	NH185733

APPENDIX F – MUNROS NEAR ROUTE (MOUNTAINS OVER 914M)

	height	start	summit
Sgùrr nan Clach Geala	1093m	NH163761	NH184715
Sgùrr nan Each	922m	NH163761	NH185698
Beinn Dearg	1084m	NH182852	NH259812
Cona' Mheall	978m	NH183852	NH275816
Meall nan Ceapraichean	977m	NH182852	NH257826
Eididh nan Clach Geala	927m	NH182852	NH258842
Seana Bhraigh	926m	NH182852	NH282879
Stage 6			
Conival	987m	NH251216	NH303199
Ben More Assynt	998m	NH251216	NH318202
Stage 14			
Ben Klibreck	962m	NC532271	NC585299

APPENDIX G
Distilleries en route

Stage 1

Glen Ord
Muir of Ord
IV6 7UJ
01463 872004
www.glenorddistillery.com
Produces The Singleton
Visits 10.00–17.00 every day

Stage 11

Wolfburn
Henderson Park
Thurso
KW14 7XW
01847 891051
www.wolfburn.com
Modern distillery, opened 2013
Visits 10.00, 12.00, 14.00 Mon–Fri

Dunnet Bay
Dunnet
KW14 8XD
01847 851287
www.dunnetbaydistillers.co.uk
Distils gin and vodka flavoured with local botanicals
Visits 11.00 and 14.00 Mon–Sat

Stage 12A

Old Pulteney
Huddart St
Wick
KW1 5BA
01955 602371
www.oldpulteney.com
Traditional single still distillery
Visits 10.00–17.00 Mon–Sat

Stage 13A

Clynelish
Brora
KW9 6LR
01408 623000
www.malts.com/en-gb/distilleries/clynelish
Modern distillery opened 1967, produces malt for Johnnie Walker blends
Visits 10.00–17.00 every day

Brora
3 Clynelish Rd
Brora
KW9 6LR
www.malts.com/en-gb/distilleries/brora
Mothballed 1983–2020, reactivated 2021

Stage 14/14A

Balblair
Edderton
IV19 1LB
01862 821273
www.balblair.com
Visits at 10.00 and 14.00 Mon–Fri

Glenmorangie
Tain
IV19 1PZ
01862 892477
www.glenmorangie.com
Scotland's best selling single malt
Visits Jun–Aug, daily 10.00–16.00 every 30min. Apr, May, Sep, Oct Mon–Fri 10.00–15.00 every hour

Appendix G – Distilleries en route

Stage 15A

Dalmore
Alness
IV17 0UT
01349 882362
www.thedalmore.com
New visitor centre due to open 2024

Teaninich
Alness
Produces malt for Diageo blends
Not open for visits

Glen Wyvis
Upper Docharty
Dingwall
IV15 9UF
01349 862005
www.glenwyvis.com
Modern community owned distillery that started producing gin and whisky in 2018

APPENDIX H
Useful contacts

Tourist information
www.visitscotland.com

Transport
LNER (direct rail service from England to Inverness)
cycle reservations
03457 225111
www.lner.co.uk

ScotRail (Scottish national railway company)
cycle reservations
03448 110141
www.scotrail.co.uk

Caledonian sleeper (overnight train from London to Inverness)
reservations
03300 600500
www.sleeper.scot

Far North Bus
0778 211 0007
www.thedurnessbus.com

Ticket to Ride (Inverness to Ullapool, Durness and John o' Groats mini-bus)
enquiries and reservations 01463 419160
www.tickettoridehighlands.co.uk/cyclist-transport

Accommodation
Scottish Youth Hostel Association
www.hostellingscotland.org.uk

Independent Hostels Guide
www.independenthostels.co.uk

Largest hotel booking site
www.booking.com

Cycling organisation
Cycling UK (formerly Cyclists' Touring Club)
01483 238301
www.cyclinguk.org

Maps and guides
NC500 (official promotion agency for the route)
www.northcoast500.com

Ordnance Survey (UK national mapping agency)
www.ordnancesurvey.co.uk

Open Street Maps (downloadable maps)
www.openstreetmap.org

Stanford's
7 Mercer Walk
London
WC2E 9FA
0207 836 1321
www.stanfords.co.uk

The Map Shop
15 High St
Upton upon Severn
WR8 0HJ
08000 854080 or 01684 593146
www.themapshop.co.uk

NOTES

DOWNLOAD THE ROUTES IN GPX FORMAT

All the routes in this guide are available for download from:

www.cicerone.co.uk/1219/GPX

as standard format GPX files. You should be able to load them into most online GPX systems and mobile devices, whether GPS or smartphone. You may need to convert the file into your preferred format using a conversion programme such as gpsvisualizer.com or one of the many other such websites and programmes.

When you follow this link, you will be asked for your email address and where you purchased the guidebook, and have the option to subscribe to the Cicerone e-newsletter.

www.cicerone.co.uk

LISTING OF CICERONE GUIDES

BRITISH ISLES CHALLENGES, COLLECTIONS AND ACTIVITIES

Cycling Land's End to John o' Groats
Great Walks on the England Coast Path
The Big Rounds
The Book of the Bivvy
The Book of the Bothy
The Mountains of England and Wales: Vol 1 Wales
The Mountains of England and Wales: Vol 2 England
The National Trails
Walking the End to End Trail

SHORT WALKS SERIES

Short Walks Hadrian's Wall
Short Walks in Arnside and Silverdale
Short Walks in Cornwall: Falmouth and the Lizard
Short Walks in Dumfries and Galloway
Short Walks in Nidderdale
Short Walks in Pembrokeshire: Tenby and the south
Short Walks in the South Downs: Brighton, Eastbourne and Arundel
Short Walks in the Surrey Hills
Short Walks Lake District – Coniston and Langdale
Short Walks Lake District: Keswick, Borrowdale and Buttermere
Short Walks Lake District: Windermere Ambleside and Grasmere
Short Walks on the Malvern Hills
Short Walks Winchester

SCOTLAND

Ben Nevis and Glen Coe
Cycling in the Hebrides
Cycling the North Coast 500
Great Mountain Days in Scotland
Mountain Biking in Southern and Central Scotland
Mountain Biking in West and North West Scotland
Not the West Highland Way
Scotland
Scotland's Best Small Mountains
Scotland's Mountain Ridges
Scottish Wild Country Backpacking
Skye's Cuillin Ridge Traverse
The Borders Abbeys Way
The Great Glen Way
The Great Glen Way Map Booklet
The Hebridean Way
The Hebrides
The Isle of Mull
The Isle of Skye
The Skye Trail
The Southern Upland Way
The West Highland Way
The West Highland Way Map Booklet
Walking Ben Lawers, Rannoch and Atholl
Walking in the Cairngorms
Walking in the Pentland Hills
Walking in the Scottish Borders
Walking in the Southern Uplands
Walking in Torridon, Fisherfield, Fannichs and An Teallach
Walking Loch Lomond and the Trossachs
Walking on Arran
Walking on Harris and Lewis
Walking on Jura, Islay and Colonsay
Walking on Rum and the Small Isles
Walking on the Orkney and Shetland Isles
Walking on Uist and Barra
Walking the Cape Wrath Trail
Walking the Corbetts
  Vol 1 South of the Great Glen
  Vol 2 North of the Great Glen
Walking the Galloway Hills
Walking the John o' Groats Trail
Walking the Munros
  Vol 1 – Southern, Central and Western Highlands
  Vol 2 – Northern Highlands and the Cairngorms
Winter Climbs in the Cairngorms
Winter Climbs: Ben Nevis and Glen Coe

NORTHERN ENGLAND ROUTES

Cycling the Reivers Route
Cycling the Way of the Roses
Hadrian's Cycleway
Hadrian's Wall Path
Hadrian's Wall Path Map Booklet
The Coast to Coast Cycle Route
The Coast to Coast Walk
The Coast to Coast Walk Map Booklet
The Pennine Way
The Pennine Way Map Booklet
Walking the Dales Way
Walking the Dales Way Map Booklet

NORTH-EAST ENGLAND, YORKSHIRE DALES AND PENNINES

Cycling in the Yorkshire Dales
Great Mountain Days in the Pennines
Mountain Biking in the Yorkshire Dales
The Cleveland Way and the Yorkshire Wolds Way
The North York Moors
Trail and Fell Running in the Yorkshire Dales
Walking in County Durham
Walking in Northumberland
Walking in the North Pennines
Walking in the Yorkshire Dales: North and East
South and West
Walking St Cuthbert's Way
Walking St Oswald's Way and Northumberland Coast Path

NORTH-WEST ENGLAND AND THE ISLE OF MAN

Cycling the Pennine Bridleway
Isle of Man Coastal Path
The Lancashire Cycleway
The Lune Valley and Howgills
Walking in Cumbria's Eden Valley
Walking in Lancashire
Walking in the Forest of Bowland and Pendle
Walking on the Isle of Man
Walking on the West Pennine Moors
Walking the Ribble Way
Walks in Silverdale and Arnside

LAKE DISTRICT

Bikepacking in the Lake District
Cycling in the Lake District
Great Mountain Days in the Lake District
Joss Naylor's Lakes, Meres and Waters of the Lake District
Lake District Winter Climbs
Lake District:
  High Level and Fell Walks
  Low Level and Lake Walks
Mountain Biking in the Lake District
Outdoor Adventures with Children – Lake District
Scrambles in the Lake District – North
South
Trail and Fell Running in the Lake District
Walking The Cumbria Way
Walking the Lake District Fells –
  Borrowdale
  Buttermere
  Coniston
  Keswick
  Langdale
  Mardale and the Far East
  Patterdale
  Wasdale
Walking the Tour of the Lake District

DERBYSHIRE, PEAK DISTRICT AND MIDLANDS

Cycling in the Peak District
Dark Peak Walks
Scrambles in the Dark Peak
Walking in Derbyshire
Walking in the Peak District –
  White Peak East
  White Peak West

SOUTHERN ENGLAND

20 Classic Sportive Rides in
  South East England
  South West England
Cycling in the Cotswolds
Mountain Biking on the
  North Downs
  South Downs
Suffolk Coast and Heath Walks
The Cotswold Way
The Cotswold Way Map Booklet
The Kennet and Avon Canal
The Lea Valley Walk
The North Downs Way
The North Downs Way Map
  Booklet
The Peddars Way and Norfolk
  Coast Path
The Pilgrims' Way
The Ridgeway National Trail
The Ridgeway National Trail
  Map Booklet
The South Downs Way
The South Downs Way Map
  Booklet
Thames Path
The Thames Path Map Booklet
The Two Moors Way
The Two Moors Way Map Booklet
Walking Hampshire's Test Way
Walking in Cornwall
Walking in Essex
Walking in Kent
Walking in London
Walking in Norfolk
Walking in the Chilterns
Walking in the Cotswolds
Walking in the Isles of Scilly
Walking in the New Forest
Walking in the North Wessex
  Downs
Walking on Dartmoor
Walking on Guernsey
Walking on Jersey
Walking on the Isle of Wight
Walking the Dartmoor Way
Walking the Jurassic Coast
Walking the South West Coast Path
Walking the South West Coast Path
  Map Booklets
  – Vol 1: Minehead to St Ives
  – Vol 2: St Ives to Plymouth
  – Vol 3: Plymouth to Poole
Walks in the South Downs
  National Park

WALES AND WELSH BORDERS

Cycle Touring in Wales
Cycling Lon Las Cymru
Great Mountain Days in
  Snowdonia
Hillwalking in Shropshire
Mountain Walking in Snowdonia
Offa's Dyke Path
Offa's Dyke Path Map Booklet
Ridges of Snowdonia
Scrambles in Snowdonia
Snowdonia: 30 Low-level and
  Easy Walks
  – North
  – South
The Cambrian Way
The Pembrokeshire Coast Path
The Pembrokeshire Coast Path
  Map Booklet
The Snowdonia Way
Walking Glyndwr's Way
Walking in Carmarthenshire
Walking in Pembrokeshire
Walking in the Brecon Beacons
Walking in the Forest of Dean
Walking in the Wye Valley
Walking on Gower
Walking the Severn Way
Walking the Shropshire Way
Walking the Wales Coast Path

INTERNATIONAL CHALLENGES, COLLECTIONS AND ACTIVITIES

Europe's High Points
Walking the Via Francigena
  Pilgrim Route – Part 1

AFRICA

Kilimanjaro
Walking in the Drakensberg
Walks and Scrambles in the
  Moroccan Anti-Atlas

ALPS CROSS-BORDER ROUTES

100 Hut Walks in the Alps
Alpine Ski Mountaineering
  Vol 1 – Western Alps
The Karnischer Hohenweg
The Tour of the Bernina
Trail Running – Chamonix and the
  Mont Blanc region
Trekking Chamonix to Zermatt
Trekking in the Alps
Trekking in the Silvretta and
  Ratikon Alps
Trekking Munich to Venice
Trekking the Tour du Mont Blanc
Trekking the Tour du Mont Blanc
  Map Booklet
Walking in the Alps

PYRENEES AND FRANCE/SPAIN CROSS-BORDER ROUTES

Shorter Treks in the Pyrenees
The Pyrenean Haute Route
The Pyrenees

Trekking the GR11 Trail
Walks and Climbs in the Pyrenees

AUSTRIA

Innsbruck Mountain Adventures
Trekking Austria's Adlerweg
Trekking in Austria's Hohe Tauern
Trekking in Austria's Zillertal Alps
Trekking in the Stubai Alps
Walking in Austria
Walking in the Salzkammergut:
  the Austrian Lake District

EASTERN EUROPE

The Danube Cycleway Vol 2
The High Tatras
The Mountains of Romania
Walking in Hungary

FRANCE, BELGIUM AND LUXEMBOURG

Camino de Santiago – Via
  Podiensis
Chamonix Mountain Adventures
Cycle Touring in France
Cycling London to Paris
Cycling the Canal de la Garonne
Cycling the Canal du Midi
Cycling the Route des Grandes
  Alpes
Mont Blanc Walks
Mountain Adventures in
  the Maurienne
Short Treks on Corsica
The Elbe Cycle Route
The GR5 Trail
The GR5 Trail – Benelux and
  Lorraine
The GR5 Trail – Vosges and Jura
The Grand Traverse of the
  Massif Central
The Moselle Cycle Route
The River Loire Cycle Route
The River Rhone Cycle Route
Trekking in the Vanoise
Trekking the Cathar Way
Trekking the GR10
Trekking the GR20 Corsica
Trekking the Robert Louis
  Stevenson Trail
Via Ferratas of the French Alps
Walking in Provence – East
Walking in Provence – West
Walking in the Ardennes
Walking in the Auvergne
Walking in the Brianconnais
Walking in the Dordogne
Walking in the Haute Savoie: North
Walking in the Haute Savoie: South
Walking on Corsica
Walking the Brittany Coast Path

GERMANY

Hiking and Cycling in the
  Black Forest
The Danube Cycleway Vol 1

The Rhine Cycle Route
The Westweg
Walking in the Bavarian Alps

IRELAND

The Wild Atlantic Way and Western Ireland
Walking the Wicklow Way

ITALY

Alta Via – Trekking in the Dolomites – Vols 1&2
Day Walks in the Dolomites
Italy's Grande Traversata delle Alpi
Italy's Sibillini National Park
Ski Touring and Snowshoeing in the Dolomites
The Way of St Francis
Trekking in the Apennines
Trekking the Giants' Trail: Alta Via 1 through the Italian Pennine Alps
Via Ferratas of the Italian Dolomites – Vols 1&2
Walking in Abruzzo
Walking in Italy's Cinque Terre
Walking in Italy's Stelvio National Park
Walking in Sicily
Walking in the Aosta Valley
Walking in the Dolomites
Walking in Tuscany
Walking in Umbria
Walking Lake Como and Maggiore
Walking Lake Garda and Iseo
Walking on the Amalfi Coast
Walking the Via Francigena Pilgrim Route – Parts 2&3
Walks and Treks in the Maritime Alps

MEDITERRANEAN

The High Mountains of Crete
Trekking in Greece
Walking and Trekking in Zagori
Walking and Trekking on Corfu
Walking in Cyprus
Walking on Malta
Walking on the Greek Islands – the Cyclades

NEW ZEALAND AND AUSTRALIA

Hiking the Overland Track

NORTH AMERICA

Hiking and Cycling the California Missions Trail
The John Muir Trail
The Pacific Crest Trail

SOUTH AMERICA

Aconcagua and the Southern Andes
Hiking and Biking Peru's Inca Trails
Trekking in Torres del Paine

SCANDINAVIA, ICELAND AND GREENLAND

Hiking in Norway – South
Trekking in Greenland – The Arctic Circle Trail
Trekking the Kungsleden
Walking and Trekking in Iceland

SLOVENIA, CROATIA, SERBIA, MONTENEGRO AND ALBANIA

Hiking Slovenia's Juliana Trail
Mountain Biking in Slovenia
The Islands of Croatia
The Julian Alps of Slovenia
The Mountains of Montenegro
The Peaks of the Balkans Trail
The Slovene Mountain Trail
Walking in Slovenia: The Karavanke
Walks and Treks in Croatia

SPAIN AND PORTUGAL

Camino de Santiago: Camino Frances
Coastal Walks in Andalucia
Costa Blanca Mountain Adventures
Cycling the Camino de Santiago
Cycling the Ruta Via de la Plata
Mountain Walking in Mallorca
Mountain Walking in Southern Catalunya
Portugal's Rota Vicentina
Spain's Sendero Historico: The GR1
The Andalucian Coast to Coast Walk
The Camino del Norte and Camino Primitivo
The Camino Ingles and Ruta do Mar
The Camino Portugues
The Mountains Around Nerja
The Mountains of Ronda and Grazalema
The Sierras of Extremadura
Trekking in Mallorca
Trekking in the Canary Islands
Trekking the GR7 in Andalucia
Walking and Trekking in the Sierra Nevada
Walking in Andalucia
Walking in Catalunya – Barcelona
Walking in Catalunya – Girona Pyrenees
Walking in Portugal
Walking in the Algarve
Walking in the Picos de Europa
Walking La Via de la Plata and Camino Sanabres
Walking on Gran Canaria
Walking on La Gomera and El Hierro
Walking on La Palma
Walking on Lanzarote and Fuerteventura
Walking on Madeira
Walking on Tenerife
Walking on the Azores
Walking on the Costa Blanca
Walking the Camino dos Faros

SWITZERLAND

Switzerland's Jura Crest Trail
The Swiss Alps
Tour of the Jungfrau Region
Trekking the Swiss Via Alpina
Walking in the Bernese Oberland – Jungfrau region
Walking in the Engadine – Switzerland
Walking in the Valais
Walking in Ticino
Walking in Zermatt and Saas-Fee

CHINA, JAPAN AND ASIA

Hiking and Trekking in the Japan Alps and Mount Fuji
Hiking in Hong Kong
Japan's Kumano Kodo Pilgrimage
Trekking in Tajikistan

HIMALAYA

Annapurna
8000 metres
Everest: A Trekker's Guide
Trekking in Bhutan
Trekking in Ladakh
Trekking in the Himalaya
Trekking in the Karakoram

MOUNTAIN LITERATURE

A Walk in the Clouds
Abode of the Gods
Fifty Years of Adventure
The Pennine Way – the Path, the People, the Journey
Unjustifiable Risk?
Unjustifiable Risk?

TECHNIQUES

Fastpacking
Geocaching in the UK
Map and Compass
Outdoor Photography
The Mountain Hut Book

MINI GUIDES

Alpine Flowers
Navigation
Pocket First Aid and Wilderness Medicine
Snow

For full information on all our guides, books and eBooks, visit our website:
www.cicerone.co.uk

CICERONE

Trust Cicerone to guide your next adventure, wherever it may be around the world...

Discover guides for hiking, mountain walking, backpacking, trekking, trail running, cycling and mountain biking, ski touring, climbing and scrambling in Britain, Europe and worldwide.

Connect with Cicerone online and find inspiration.

- buy books and ebooks
- articles, advice and trip reports
- podcasts and live events
- GPX files and updates
- regular newsletter

cicerone.co.uk